Thyroid Disorders

Titles in the Diseases & Disorders series include:

Acne
ADHD
Alcoholism
Allergies
Amnesia
Anorexia and Bulimia
Anxiety Disorders
Asperger's Syndrome
Autism
Blindness
Brain Trauma
Brain Tumors
Cancer
Cerebral Palsy
Cervical Cancer
Childhood Obesity
Dementia
Depression
Diabetes
Epilepsy
Hepatitis
Hodgkin's Disease

Human Papillomavirus
  (HPV)
Infectious
  Mononucleosis
Malnutrition
Mental Retardation
Migraines
MRSA
Multiple Sclerosis
Personality Disorders
Phobias
Plague
Post Traumatic Stress
  Disorder
Prostate Cancer
Sexually Transmitted
  Diseases
Skin Cancer
Speech Disorders
Sports Injuries
Sudden Infant Death
  Syndrome

DISEASES & DISORDERS

Thyroid Disorders

Bonnie Juettner

LUCENT BOOKS

A part of Gale, Cengage Learning

GALE
CENGAGE Learning

Detroit • New York • San Francisco • New Haven, Conn • Waterville, Maine • London

GALE
CENGAGE Learning™

LIBRARY OF CONGRESS CATALOGING-IN-PUBLICATION DATA

Juettner, Bonnie.
Thyroid disorders / by Bonnie Juettner.
   p. cm. -- (Diseases & disorders)
  Includes bibliographical references and index.
  ISBN 978-1-4205-0223-7 (hardcover)
  1. Thyroid gland--Diseases. I. Title.
  RC655.J82 2010
  616.4'4--dc22

                                                    2010004753

Lucent Books
27500 Drake Rd.
Farmington Hills, MI 48331

ISBN-13: 978-1-4205-0223-7
ISBN-10: 1-4205-0223-9

Printed in the United States of America
1 2 3 4 5 6 7 14 13 12 11 10

Printed by Bang Printing, Brainerd, MN, 1ˢᵗ Ptg., 05/2010

Table of Contents

Foreword   6

Introduction
    A Hidden Cause of Fatigue   8

Chapter One
    The Speed Control for the Body   14

Chapter Two
    Hypothyroidism: An Underactive Thyroid   30

Chapter Three
    Hyperthyroidism: An Overactive Thyroid   46

Chapter Four
    Thyroid Nodules and Thyroid Cancer   63

Chapter Five
    The Future of Thyroid Research: Brain Chemistry   81

Notes   98
Glossary   101
Organizations to Contact   103
For Further Reading   105
Index   107
Picture Credits   111
About the Author   112

"The Most Difficult Puzzles Ever Devised"

Charles Best, one of the pioneers in the search for a cure for diabetes, once explained what it is about medical research that intrigued him so. "It's not just the gratification of knowing one is helping people," he confided, "although that probably is a more heroic and selfless motivation. Those feelings may enter in, but truly, what I find best is the feeling of going toe to toe with nature, of trying to solve the most difficult puzzles ever devised. The answers are there somewhere, those keys that will solve the puzzle and make the patient well. But how will those keys be found?"

Since the dawn of civilization, nothing has so puzzled people—and often frightened them, as well—as the onset of illness in a body or mind that had seemed healthy before. A seizure, the inability of a heart to pump, the sudden deterioration of muscle tone in a small child—being unable to reverse such conditions or even to understand why they occur was unspeakably frustrating to healers. Even before there were names for such conditions, even before they were understood at all, each was a reminder of how complex the human body was, and how vulnerable.

While our grappling with understanding diseases has been frustrating at times, it has also provided some of humankind's most heroic accomplishments. Alexander Fleming's accidental discovery in 1928 of a mold that could be turned into penicillin has resulted in the saving of untold millions of lives. The isolation of the enzyme insulin has reversed what was once a death sentence for anyone with diabetes. There have been great strides in combating conditions for which there is not yet a cure, too. Medicines can help AIDS patients live longer, diagnostic tools such as mammography and ultrasounds can help doctors find tumors while they are treatable, and laser surgery techniques have made the most intricate, minute operations routine.

This "toe-to-toe" competition with diseases and disorders is even more remarkable when seen in a historical continuum. An astonishing amount of progress has been made in a very short time. Just two hundred years ago, the existence of germs as a cause of some diseases was unknown. In fact, it was less than 150 years ago that a British surgeon named Joseph Lister had difficulty persuading his fellow doctors that washing their hands before delivering a baby might increase the chances of a healthy delivery (especially if they had just attended to a diseased patient)!

Each book in Lucent's Diseases and Disorders series explores a disease or disorder and the knowledge that has been accumulated (or discarded) by doctors through the years. Each book also examines the tools used for pinpointing a diagnosis, as well as the various means that are used to treat or cure a disease. Finally, new ideas are presented—techniques or medicines that may be on the horizon.

Frustration and disappointment are still part of medicine, for not every disease or condition can be cured or prevented. But the limitations of knowledge are being pushed outward constantly; the "most difficult puzzles ever devised" are finding challengers every day.

A Hidden Cause of Fatigue

"I was . . . feeling tired, really tired, going around from doctor to doctor trying to figure out what was wrong," talk show host Oprah Winfrey told her audience in 2007. "I finally figured out that I had literally sort of blew out my thyroid."[1]

The thyroid is a small gland located in the throat, just below the larynx, or voice box. It is wrapped around the windpipe on

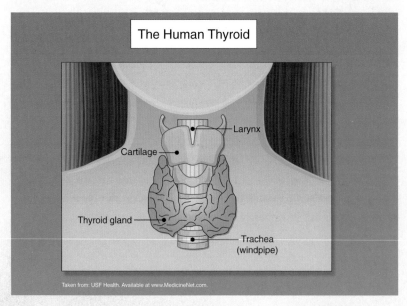

The Human Thyroid

Larynx

Cartilage

Thyroid gland

Trachea (windpipe)

Taken from: USF Health. Available at www.MedicineNet.com.

three sides. The ancient Greeks thought that the thyroid gland looked like a shield, so they named it "shield-shaped." (The English word for *thyroid* is derived from the Greek word for *shield-shaped*.) The Adam's apple is made of thyroid cartilage, but the thyroid gland is below the Adam's apple. Most people never notice it unless it swells from infection or they develop a goiter (an enlarged thyroid gland).

The Endocrine System

The thyroid gland, along with other glands in the body, is part of the endocrine system. This means that it makes hormones. The endocrine system can be hard to understand. It does not work in ways that are obvious to most people, the way some of the body's other systems do. The endocrine system is harder to understand because people cannot see it or feel it in everyday life—they can only see its effects.

The hormones made by the endocrine system are chemicals that travel throughout the body. These chemicals stimulate growth and development, and they help to keep the body in balance. An imbalance in hormone levels can cause all kinds of symptoms, such as feeling dizzy or nauseated, feeling tired and sleepy, finding it difficult to concentrate, or finding it hard to fall asleep. (Puberty and pregnancy as well are governed by hormones—but these conditions are not disorders, just a normal part of human growth and development.)

Thyroid disorders are one kind of hormone imbalance. But there are others, too, such as diabetes. This is a disease that develops when the pancreas, a gland connected to the digestive system, does not make enough insulin—a hormone that removes sugar from the blood and helps the body to make use of it.

When Winfrey began to feel tired all the time, the last thing she thought about was the possibility that she might have a hormone imbalance. Instead, she concluded that she must be working too hard and that she needed to get more rest, get some exercise, and eat a nutritious diet. She tried taking better care of herself, which would have helped if her tiredness had been normal exhaustion from overwork. But Winfrey's fatigue

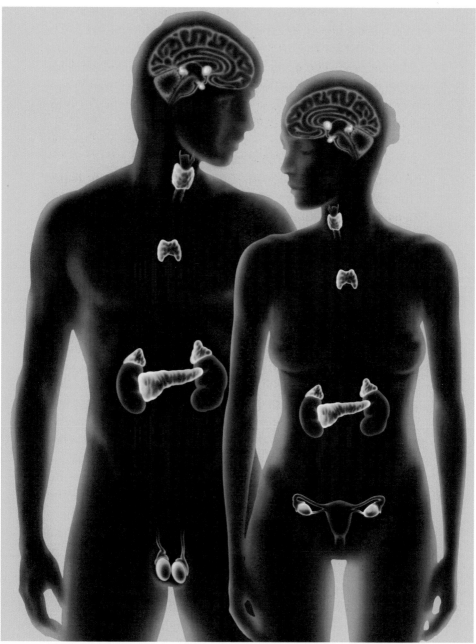

The endocrine systems of a man and woman are depicted in this illustration. From top to bottom: the hypothalamus, pineal gland, hypophysis, thyroid gland, thymus, suprarenal glands, pancreas, and ovaries (female) and testes (male).

would not lift, no matter how much rest she got. At that point she decided to see a doctor. It was a good decision. People often do not think to go to the doctor just because they are tired. But when fatigue reaches the point that a person is tired upon waking up, tired after simple activities like grocery shopping, too tired to work, and too tired to exercise, it is likely that the cause is something more than just lack of rest.

Unfortunately, many different medical reasons might make a person feel tired. Winfrey had to go to several doctors and rule out other diagnoses, but she eventually found out what was wrong. "My body was turning on me," she said later. "First hyperthyroidism, which sped up my metabolism and left me unable to sleep for days. (Most people lose weight. I didn't.) Then hypothyroidism, which slowed down my metabolism and made me want to sleep all the time. (Most people gain weight. I did! Twenty pounds.)"[2]

Suffering in Silence

Winfrey is not alone. Every year more than 20 million Americans are treated for thyroid disorders. Endocrinologists, doctors who specialize in hormone disorders, estimate that another 14 million Americans live with thyroid disorders that have never been diagnosed. They hypothesize that one out of every ten Americans has a thyroid problem. The problem has become so widespread that the American Association of Clinical Endocrinologists has begun to advocate free public screenings for thyroid diseases.

Thyroid disorders can affect people of any age, even newborns. But the majority of thyroid patients are women between the ages of thirty and fifty. Women are about ten times more likely to develop thyroid disorders than men. About one out of every eight women will develop a thyroid disorder at some point in her lifetime. The likelihood of developing a thyroid disorder increases with age. About 10 percent of women over the age of forty have an undiagnosed thyroid disorder. Among sixty-year-old women, nearly 17 percent have hypothyroidism, an underactive thyroid.

Vague Symptoms

Thyroid disorders are fairly common, and they can be diagnosed by taking a medical history and following up with a
blood test. Yet thyroid disorders often remain undiagnosed for
years at a time. One reason is that the symptoms can be vague.
British radio talk show host Chessy Nand had a bout with thyroid disease that began when she was twenty-one. A year earlier she had experienced a traumatic loss when her boyfriend
and her best friend both died in a motorbike accident. Nand,
pulling her life back together, began working on a college degree in business studies and suddenly gained so much weight
that she doubled her dress size in four months. She began having panic attacks, and her neck became swollen. She felt
groggy all the time. Nand later wrote: "Mum later told me how
we were eating dinner together one night when she saw my
eyes glaze over. I sat with my fork in the air, staring into space.
She said it looked as if my batteries had run down."[3]

Nand's symptoms were so vague that she and her family had
some doubts about whether she was really sick. They wondered if she might simply be having a hard time adjusting to
her boyfriend's death. She went to her primary care doctor, but
the doctor told her she was fine and that she just needed to exercise and lose weight. She tried, but she was too tired to exercise. After a year she went to see a specialist and had the levels
of thyroid hormones in her blood tested. She found out that
she had an underactive thyroid. After several months of treatment with thyroid hormone replacement medication, she began to feel as if she were getting her life back. She lost weight,
regained her mental sharpness, stopped having panic attacks,
and finished her degree. Nand's voice was left permanently
husky from the damage to her thyroid, but the damage did not
stop her from pursuing a career as a radio journalist.

Thyroid disorders are not always easy to diagnose. Many patients go from doctor to doctor, as Winfrey did, trying to figure
out what could be wrong. Patients may feel uncomfortable list-
ing for their doctors symptoms that seem odd and unrelated:
dry skin, heart palpitations, anxiety, fatigue, irritability, consti-

Thyroid disorders are fairly easy to detect with a medical exam and blood test but they can remain undiagnosed for years.

pation, hair loss, weight gain, nerve damage such as carpal tunnel syndrome . . . the list is almost endless. Patients with so many different symptoms in so many different parts of the body may start to feel that they are going crazy or overreacting. They may fear that the doctor will regard them as hypochondriacs. Or they may simply feel as though their bodies are falling apart. Fortunately, however, once doctors are alerted to the possibility of a thyroid disorder, they can screen for it with a simple blood test. Once a disorder is discovered, it is usually fairly simple to treat—and patients can get back to leading a normal life again.

CHAPTER ONE

The Speed Control for the Body

The thyroid gland is part of the endocrine system—the system that controls hormones. The endocrine system is one of the body's major organ systems. There are ten more. The others are the circulatory system, the digestive system, the excretory system, the immune system, the integumentary system, the lymphatic system, the muscular system, the nervous system, the respiratory system, and the skeletal system.

Organ Systems

Each organ system is made up of two or more organs. Organs are made up of tissues—groups of cells, all of which work together to do a particular job. Each organ system has a different job in the body. The work of some organ systems is obvious. The digestive system digests food. It includes the mouth, esophagus, stomach, and intestines. The circulatory system circulates blood throughout the body. Its major organs are the heart and blood vessels. The respiratory system includes the nose and sinuses, parts of the throat, and the lungs. It processes the air that people breathe.

The work of some other systems, though, is not so obvious. For example, the nervous system includes the brain, spinal cord, and nerves. It controls thoughts and emotions. It regulates the work of other organ systems. The nerves of the nervous system carry information back and forth throughout the entire body, forming a network that is physically connected to the brain and the spinal column. But the nervous system does its work invisibly.

The endocrine system works invisibly, too. Like the nervous system, the endocrine system is a communication network. It transports information. But the nervous system sends information through a vast network of nerves. The organs of the endocrine system, however, are not physically connected to each other. The organs of the endocrine system are the glands. Humans have many glands located all over the body. Instead of communicating with each other through a network the way the nervous system does, the glands communicate by sending chemical messages. The chemical messages released by the glands are called hormones.

Hormones

Each hormone has a special function. When a gland releases hormones, it deposits the hormones into the bloodstream, where they can travel through the body. As the blood carries hormones past different cells in the body, the hormones happen to touch some of the cells. Certain of these cells have receptors, places where the hormone can connect to the cell and stimulate it to take different actions. If a cell does not have a receptor for a particular hormone, the hormone passes it by and continues to travel in the blood. If the cell does have a receptor, the hormone sticks to it. Some doctors compare cell receptors and hormones to locks and keys. Each "key," or hormone, can only stick to a certain type of "lock," or cell receptor. Once it is there, the hormone can stimulate the cell to do certain things, such as make a particular protein or enzyme.

Among the glands that regulate the body through hormones are the adrenal glands, which are above the kidneys. When a person is suddenly startled or frightened, the adrenal glands release hormones that target cells in the nervous system. When these hormones connect to the receptors on nerve cells, they cause the entire nervous system to snap to attention. The brain

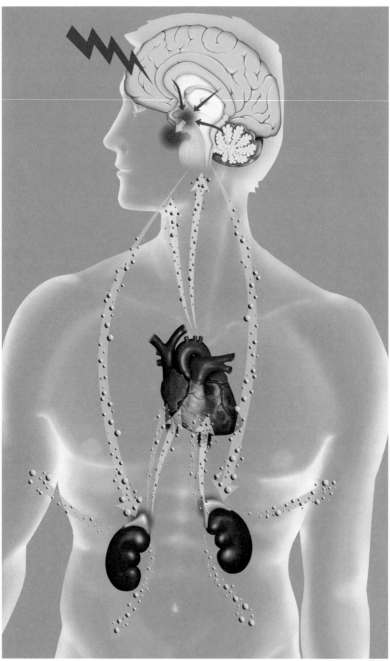

When the body reacts to stress (red), the hypothalamus stimulates the hypophysis to release hormones (green) which in turn stimulate the suprarenal gland to secrete adredalin (yellow) and cortisol (blue).

becomes alert and ready to react to any danger. Likewise, the thymus gland, in the chest, releases hormones when the body is experiencing a viral or bacterial infection. Hormones from the thymus connect to receptors on white blood cells. They stimulate the white blood cells to mature faster in order to fight the infection (the thymus is part of the immune system as well as the endocrine system). Puberty and pregnancy, as well, are regulated by the action of hormones. During these stages of life, the pituitary gland releases hormones that stimulate cells in the reproductive organs to grow and develop in certain ways.

Governing the Metabolism

The thyroid gland is different from the adrenal glands, the thymus, and the reproductive organs, however. In some ways the thyroid gland is more similar to organs such as the heart, the lungs, and the brain because, like those organs, the thyroid gland affects the entire body. The thyroid does not only respond to a special or unusual set of events such as infection, stress, or puberty. It also performs actions that affect every part of the body all the time. When thyroid hormones stick to receptors on cells, they do not stimulate cells to perform a specific action. Instead, they speed up all the cells' activities.

The speed at which cells operate is part of the body's metabolism, which is governed by the thyroid gland. Metabolism is how the body gets its energy, which sounds like a simple concept. But human metabolism is extremely complicated, because the human body is so complex. Every cell, every tissue, every organ, and every organ system in the body needs energy. To get energy, cells must use chemical processes to break down certain materials and put together others. Cells can break down and build up materials quickly or slowly, depending on the thyroid.

Producing Energy

Organ systems can break down materials into chemicals that give the body energy. For example, digestion breaks food down into nutrients. Respiration breaks air down into the particular molecules that humans need. Digestion and respiration, though, are just the beginning of the process of human metabolism.

Iodized Salt

Like all the body's organs, the thyroid gland needs fuel to do its work. The fuel used by the thyroid gland is iodine. People who do not get enough iodine in their diets can develop underactive thyroids, or hypothyroidism. Worldwide, more than 1 billion people have hypothyroidism caused by iodine deficiency. In children, iodine deficiency is one of the main causes of mental retardation. When women do not get enough iodine during pregnancy, their babies may be born with a severe form of iodine deficiency called cretinism, which causes gross mental retardation, short stature, deafness, mutism, and a tendency toward spastic movements.

However, in the United States iodine deficiency is rare. That is because during World War I, army doctors noticed that many of their new recruits from the Midwest had developed goiters, or swollen thyroids. Often those goiters were the first symptoms of iodine deficiency. To prevent hypothyroidism, the United States began adding iodine to milk, bread, and salt, to make sure that everyone was getting enough of it.

An infant shows the effects of hypothyroidism, an iodine deficiency. Iodine deficiencies in infants are one of the leading causes of mental retardation.

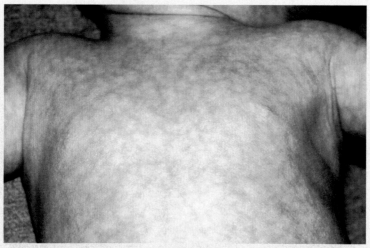

They provide the raw materials such as glucose (a sugar molecule) and oxygen that the body can use to make energy. Once glucose and oxygen have been released into the blood, the circulatory system can transport them to the body's cells.

The body's cells cannot use glucose and oxygen as they are, however. Cells convert glucose and oxygen into a form of energy that they can use. Then they excrete waste—the substances they do not need—into the blood and the lymph fluid. This waste is carried away by the circulatory and lymphatic systems. Then it is eliminated by the excretory system, in the urine and sweat.

Speed Control for Cells

The human body's metabolism, therefore, includes the activities of all the body's organ systems and the activities of every organ, tissue, and cell. The thyroid gland can speed up any or all of these processes—or, if it does not release enough hormones, it can slow them all down. "If you think of the body as a machine," says Mario Skugor of the Cleveland Clinic, "thyroid hormones control the rate at which the machine runs."[4] Psychiatrist Jim Phelps agrees, explaining that thyroid hormone

> sets your "idle," rather like a car mechanic sets the idle of your car by adjusting the carburetor. If your thyroid level is set too high, you burn a lot of energy even sitting still. . . .
>
> If thyroid hormone is too low . . . you don't burn much energy except when active. It's as if your "carburetor" is set to idle too low: when you stop doing something, you practically turn off completely.[5]

Because it controls the speed of the body's operations, the thyroid can affect the rate at which the heart beats and the speed of digestion. It even determines the speed of operations in the brain—which means that a healthy thyroid can make a big difference in how fast a person thinks, talks, and works.

Growth and Development

By controlling the metabolism, the thyroid also governs growth and development. It can cause a developing child to grow more quickly or more slowly than normal. As a result, having a healthy thyroid gland is especially important for babies and children. Children with healthy thyroids grow at a normal pace and hit their developmental milestones at regular intervals. Children with thyroid disorders, however, may not develop normally. They may be much smaller than other children of the same age, or much taller. Fortunately, thyroid disorders are rare among U.S. children. Worldwide, though, hypothyroidism caused by iodine deficiency is one of the major causes of mental retardation in children. (Thyroid hormones are made out of iodine.) Iodine deficiency is rare in the United States because the country adds iodine to salt.

Hormones relating to growth and development affect adults, too. They stimulate the formation of new cells and tissue in the heart, brain, eyes, skin, muscle, bone, liver, kidneys, and intestines. They also stimulate the body's cells to reproduce themselves when necessary to repair damaged or infected tissues.

How Thyroid Hormones Work

The thyroid gland works the same way other glands work: It releases hormones into the bloodstream and the blood carries the hormones throughout the body. The thyroid does not act on its own to release thyroid hormones, however. Like all the other organs in the body, the thyroid gland takes its instructions from the brain. Although the glands of the endocrine system are not physically connected to each other, they are connected to the nervous system through the brain. The connection is located in a gland called the hypothalamus. The hypothalamus is located in the middle of the brain. The hypothalamus is part of both the nervous system and the endocrine system. As a member of the nervous system, it receives information from sensory organs such as the skin. As a member of the endocrine system, it produces master hormones that tell the body's other glands what hormones they should release.

The hormones produced by the hypothalamus do not travel directly to the body's glands, however. Instead, they travel through a series of short blood vessels to a nearby gland at the

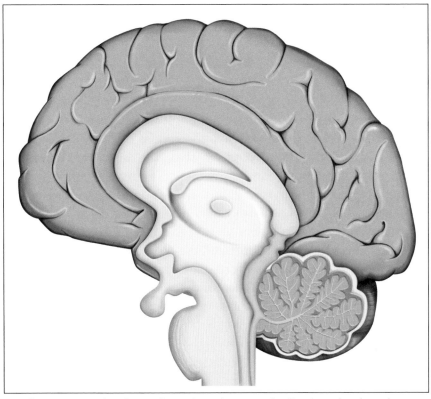

The pituitary gland, in yellow, directly controls all other glands in the body.

base of the brain. This gland, the pituitary, is the direct supervisor for all the other glands in the body. The brain constantly monitors conditions in the body and reacts when conditions (such as skin temperature or blood sugar levels) become unfavorable. The hypothalamus and pituitary continually adjust and readjust the amounts of hormones they release, trying to keep the body's operating conditions consistently within a certain range.

When the pituitary gland receives hormonal signals from the hypothalamus, it releases its own hormones directly into the bloodstream. Hormones from the pituitary travel directly to the body's other glands. For example, the pituitary gland responds to rising levels of sugar in the bloodstream by sending hormonal signals to the pancreas, stimulating it to release insulin and glucagon, hormones that regulate the concentration of sugar in the blood.

Thyroid-Stimulating Hormone

The hormone that the pituitary gland sends to the thyroid is called thyroid-stimulating hormone (TSH). The pituitary does not release TSH on its own, though. It waits to receive TSH-releasing hormone from the hypothalamus.

After the pituitary releases TSH, the hormone travels through the bloodstream to the neck. The receptors for TSH are all within the thyroid gland. TSH enters the thyroid and binds to receptors on thyroid cells. There it stimulates them to release thyroxine, a hormone that it is made of iodine molecules. Thyroxine travels through the bloodstream, sticking to appropriate receptors as it reaches them, just as other hormones do. When thyroid hormones stick to a cell's receptors, they stimulate the cell to speed up, working faster and becoming more active. The cells begin to use more nutrients, breaking the nutrients down into energy.

Staying in Balance

As the body's cells speed up, breaking down oxygen and glucose to make energy, a person should start to feel warmer, more alert, and more energetic. When a person's thyroid hormones are in balance and the person is not suffering from any diseases or disorders, the person should feel fairly good. The body's organ systems should be working at their optimum speeds. The heart should beat steadily and not palpitate (beat rapidly). Blood pressure should be normal. Digestion should proceed at a normal pace, with no diarrhea and no constipation. The person should feel mentally and emotionally balanced, able to think clearly, pay attention, learn new things, and adapt to changing events. All other things being equal, the body should be feeling and operating at its best.

Often, all other things are not equal. People whose overall health, including the health of the endocrine system, has been weakened may have a harder time staying in balance. They may be more likely to develop heart problems, high or low blood pressure, or digestive difficulties. They could also find it more difficult to focus mentally, feel scattered or forgetful, or become moody and irritable. They might have persistent aches and pains or have a hard time staying warm enough or cool enough. Signs of imbalance such as these suggest that the body has been weakened in some way and is not functioning at its peak efficiency. The reason could be something simple such as hunger, lack of sleep, high stress levels, poor nutrition, or infection with a cold or flu virus. Or the reason might be something more complex, such as a disruption of one of the body's organ systems or one of the body's organs, such as the thyroid gland.

Feeling out of balance and having vague symptoms does not necessarily suggest to a doctor that a patient may have a thyroid disorder. The thyroid gland is just one of the organs that needs to be kept healthy and strong if the body is going to remain in balance and function well. But many doctors have come to believe that thyroid health is one of the baseline indicators of health that health care professionals should routinely monitor in their patients.

Thyroid Screening

Thyroid disorders can be difficult to recognize, even for a doctor. The symptoms can be very vague. Because thyroid hormones affect the entire body, symptoms of a thyroid disorder can show up in any or all of the body's organs and organ systems. The earliest symptoms may be subtle things that only a very sensitive person would notice. Sometimes a doctor may have a patient whose only symptom is that he or she just does not feel good. The doctor may suspect that nothing is wrong with the patient at all and that the disorder, if there is one, is entirely mental or emotional. In fact, sometimes the earliest symptoms of a thyroid disorder are purely psychological. Many thyroid patients do not even go to the doctor at first.

Because it is so hard to diagnose thyroid disorders based on the symptoms, some doctors are taking the approach of routinely ordering a blood test to check the thyroid hormone levels of patients who fall into certain categories. For instance, newborns are always checked for hypothyroidism, not because they

Goiters

Most symptoms of thyroid disorders are vague and hard to diagnose because they can be caused by so many other disorders as well. Goiters, however, are an unmistakable sign of a thyroid problem. A goiter is the term people use to refer to a thyroid gland that has swollen to an abnormal size. Sometimes the whole gland swells, while other times only part of it becomes enlarged. Goiters can be symptoms of either underactive or overactive thyroids.

Treatment of hypothyroidism or hyperthyroidism may cause a goiter to shrink—or the goiter may remain as it is. Either way, goiters are not a sign of thyroid cancer; they are always benign. However, a goiter may have nodules growing on it. If so, it is called a multinodular goiter. In older people the nodules on multinodular goiters frequently produce large amounts of thyroid hormone, causing hyperthyroidism. This type of hyperthyroidism is fairly easy to diagnose, because a doctor can feel the bumpy goiter in a neck exam.

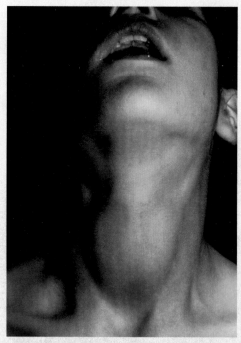

Goiters are caused by a swelling of the thyroid gland and are usually benign.

are at more risk, but because untreated hypothyroidism is so dangerous for babies. People who have a family history of thyroid disease or a family history of an autoimmune disorder such as diabetes, lupus, or rheumatoid arthritis are also routinely screened for thyroid problems because they are more at risk for developing thyroid disorders themselves. Many gynecologists also routinely order thyroid panels as part of their annual checkup for women over the age of thirty, knowing that women are much more likely to develop thyroid disorders than men and that a woman's chances of developing a thyroid disorder increase with age. Some psychiatrists also routinely check thyroid function in their patients, since thyroid disorders are a common cause of depression, anxiety, and other mood disorders. Once the possibility of a thyroid disorder has been raised, it is much easier for doctors to diagnose a patient's problem.

Blood Tests

Doctors used to diagnose thyroid disorders based on a patient's medical history and symptoms. But now it is possible to test a patient's blood for thyroid hormones. Many doctors feel that the most sensitive blood test for thyroid disease is a TSH test—a test of the levels of thyroid-stimulating hormone released by the pituitary gland. Patients who have an underactive thyroid, or hypothyroidism, will normally have higher than average levels of TSH in their blood because the pituitary releases more and more TSH in an attempt to stimulate an underactive thyroid. On the other hand, patients who have an overactive thyroid, or hyperthyroidism, will normally have much lower than normal levels of TSH in their blood because the pituitary will stop trying to stimulate a thyroid gland that is already too active.

Doctors can follow up on abnormal TSH results by testing the blood levels of hormones that are made by the thyroid: thyroxine, called T_4, and triiodothyronine, called T_3. (These hormones are called T_3 and T_4 because they contain iodine atoms—three iodine atoms in T_3 and four in T_4). If TSH levels are high and doctors suspect hypothyroidism, they would expect to find low levels of T_3 and T_4. If TSH levels are low and doctors suspect hyperthyroidism, they would expect to find high levels of T_3 and T_4. Thus, tests of T_3 and T_4 levels can be used to confirm an initial diagnosis.

What Is Normal?

Even with blood test results, thyroid disorders can sometimes be difficult to diagnose. Tests of TSH, T_3, and T_4 levels have only been around for about thirty years. Doctors are still trying to determine what levels of these hormones in the blood should be considered normal. Laboratories keep changing the ranges that are classified as normal. For hypothyroidism, for example, the normal range has been moving up. T_3 and T_4 levels that used to be classified at the low end of normal are now considered hypothyroid. Some patients have been told by doctor after doctor that they had normal levels of thyroid hormones, only to be told later that in light of new information and new research, they seem to have been suffering from undiagnosed hypothyroidism for years. That is what happened to fifty-four-year-old Mary, who later wrote about her experience:

> My first symptoms . . . were depression and fatigue. Prozac overcame the depression but not the chronic tiredness.
>
> Every doctor's visit yielded a different diagnosis. Severe cramps and constipation were labeled diverticulosis . . . when my hair started falling out in clumps, the doctor said the cause was stress . . . after two emergency room visits, I was referred to a rheumologist, who promptly diagnosed rheumatoid arthritis. . . . Only once did a doctor order a thyroid screening—after I mentioned having gained twenty pounds (from 105 to 125) in six months. The TSH was elevated according to today's guidelines but at that time was considered "high normal."[6]

Doctors who specialize in thyroid disorders have come to realize that they must be very careful in how they interpret blood test results, especially when the results are normal but are at the low end or high end of the normal range.

Doctors diagnose thyroid disorders with the use of a blood analysis machine that verifies that the thyroid gland is functioning properly.

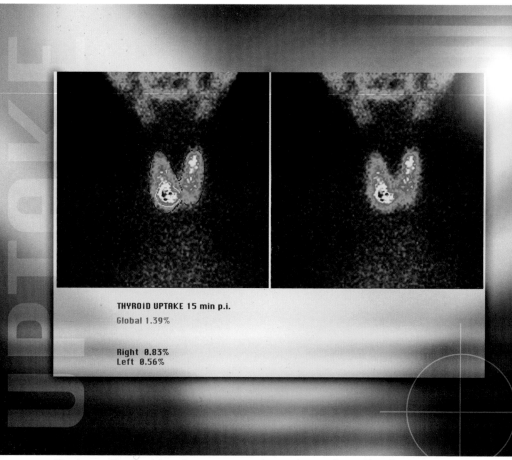

THYROID UPTAKE 15 min p.i.
Global 1.39%

Right 0.83%
Left 0.56%

If a doctor finds a blood test is inconclusive, he or she will order a radioactive uptake scan which can determine how much iodine the thyroid is collecting.

More Tests

If blood tests are inconclusive, doctors can order other tests. One option is a radioactive iodine uptake scan. One of the thyroid's jobs in the body is to collect and store iodine. The thyroid needs iodine because thyroid hormones are made out of it. If a patient takes a dose of radioactive iodine, the thyroid will collect it, and a few hours later, technicians can take a scan of the thyroid using a tool that measures radioactivity. The scan shows how much iodine was collected by the thyroid.

A lower-than-normal uptake indicates that the thyroid is underactive, while a higher-than-normal uptake indicates a hyperactive thyroid.

Fortunately for people with a thyroid disorder, such disorders are relatively simple to treat once they have been diagnosed. Most patients can be treated with thyroid hormones. Many may find that they have to give their bodies time to adjust to the changes in their hormone levels. After a few months, though, patients often find that they feel much better. Fatigue and mental fog lift, moods tend to improve, and the odd, random symptoms such as constipation and hair loss start to clear up.

Doctors who specialize in thyroid disorders often find it very satisfying to treat patients who have been trying for months or years to figure out what was wrong with them. Kenneth Ain, the director of the University of Kentucky Thyroid Clinic, explains that he became interested in the thyroid when he was a new intern working in the intensive care unit of a hospital. He writes: "As a new intern, my first intensive care patient was a comatose gentleman whose illness had defied understanding for three weeks. What a triumph for a new physician to diagnose myxedema (hypothyroid) coma and see my patient awaken after sufficient treatment with thyroid hormone!"[7]

CHAPTER TWO

Hypothyroidism: An Underactive Thyroid

Jennifer, a twenty-two-year-old college student, had reached a time in her life when she should have been full of energy. Instead, she felt tired all the time and had lost the stamina she needed to exercise. "I constantly feel drained, as if I could doze off at any moment," she observed at the time. "Even with nine hours' sleep, I feel like I stayed up all night. . . . After a bike ride the other day, I was shaking and so weak I could barely hold a glass of water! Even standing for a couple of hours makes me feel like I'm going to pass out."[8] Jennifer was cold all the time, too. On a warm September day, she needed to blast the heat in her car to feel warm. Her hands and feet felt cold all the time.

Diagnosing Hypothyroidism

Jennifer went to her doctor, who decided to check the levels of TSH, thyroid-stimulating hormone, in her blood. Jennifer's TSH was unusually high. A normal TSH result for her would have been between 0.4 and 5.5 units of TSH per milliliter of blood. But Jennifer's TSH was over 100. When TSH levels are so high, doctors surmise that the thyroid is not working well. They hypothesize that the pituitary gland is sending out higher amounts of TSH to try to jump-start the thyroid into functioning properly. It seemed likely that Jennifer had hypothyroidism—an underactive thyroid. Her thyroid was not releasing enough thyroid hormones.

Marie, like Jennifer, started to feel the effects of hypothyroidism in college. Like Jennifer, Marie was exhausted. She found it very difficult to concentrate on her work. Unlike Jennifer, though, Marie did not see a doctor. She assumed that she was tired because she was a nursing student and had to work long hours at a local hospital in order to finish her clinical training. Marie also had another common symptom of hypothyroidism: anxiety. She later wrote:

> I was so afraid that I would not pass my exams, that I would be a failure. . . I had myself so worked up and anxious that one of my college professors called me and said,

One of the symptoms of hypothyroidism is a constant feeling of fatigue.

"What is going on? You're not yourself." I told her I was fine, but I was just a ball of nerves. She said, "No, you're not yourself. You are normally very calm. Now, you seem to be running on adrenaline." I told her it must be the anxiety of having to take tests.[9]

Although Marie was a nursing student, she did not think she needed to see a doctor. Her symptoms, fatigue and anxiety, seemed like something she should be able to handle herself. She suffered with her symptoms for two years before she finally mentioned them to her doctor. After she was diagnosed and treated for hypothyroidism, she began to feel much better. After four months of treatment, her thyroid test results returned to normal, her anxiety greatly diminished, and she regained the ability to focus and concentrate on her work.

Slowing Everything Down

An underactive thyroid deprives the body of the levels of thyroid hormones it would normally need. Because thyroid hormones control the speed of cellular processes, lowering the levels of thyroid hormones in the blood causes the body's whole metabolism to slow down.

When the metabolism slows down, all the body's processes slow down. But the first process to slow down is the process that cells use to convert food nutrients and oxygen into energy. Slowing this process down means that the body's cells are low on energy. The entire body ends up feeling nonenergetic. As a result, fatigue is the first symptom of hypothyroidism that most people notice. It is also the most common symptom of hypothyroidism. But all the body's systems, including digestion, circulation, healing from injuries, reflexes such as the ability to move out of the way of a falling object, and mental processes such as thinking and speaking slow down, too. So fatigue is only the beginning of the symptoms that a hypothyroid person may experience.

Symptoms of Hypothyroidism

The symptoms of hypothyroidism are often so mild and vague that even though hypothyroidism is the most common thyroid disorder, it is an easy disorder to miss or to misdiagnose. Hypothyroidism usually starts with fatigue, which is a symptom of many other diseases and disorders as well. As the body slows down, people with hypothyroidism often lose their appetite and the digestion slows down, leading to constipation.

Despite their loss of appetite, however, people with hypothyroidism frequently gain weight and find it impossible to lose that weight no matter how little they eat or how much they exercise. The mother of Candace, a young woman with hypothyroidism that was undiagnosed at the time, remarked later: "We went on Jenny Craig together. The diet worked perfectly for me, but not for her. She kept cheating and didn't have the will power to do it. She was depressed and crying."[10] Finding it hard to lose weight, though, is such a common problem that most people are unlikely to think of having their thyroid checked.

In addition to digestion, other body systems slow down, too. As the circulatory system slows down, the body's ability to break down cholesterol diminishes, so many people with hypothyroidism develop high cholesterol. Many develop high blood pressure as well. The cells in the skin begin to repair wounds more slowly and the skin may become dry, thick, and itchy. Hair and fingernails may grow more slowly and be dry and brittle. Muscles may ache more.

Sometimes the symptoms of hypothyroidism can be very subtle. Indiana doctor Don Michael, who experienced hypothyroidism himself, says that the first symptom he noticed was a difference in the amount of weight he could curl during his workouts. "At the gym," Michael says, "I found that I was no longer able to curl as much weight as I used to." The symptom is a typical one but tends to show up only when athletes are used to working near the top end of their normal capacity—a difference in workouts might not even be noticed by someone whose ordinary workouts are milder and less intense. Michael did not even think of hypothyroidism when he first started having trouble with his workouts. "With the characteristic unthinking of a hypothyroid," he comments, "I just put back the weights I always used, and got a lighter set."[11]

Many people with hypothyroidism experience a decline in efficiency during a workout.

Difficulty Focusing

As the body's systems slow down, the nervous system and the brain are affected, too. People with hypothyroidism often find that they feel mentally sluggish, sleepy, and forgetful. They find it hard to focus or concentrate and begin to stop caring about whether they get anything done or not. This is what happened to Lisa, another college student who developed hypothyroidism. When she was first diagnosed, she commented:

> I have lost the ability to concentrate. I ask a question and forget the answer immediately, and I have to ask again. It is humiliating. I think of one thing and then another, and I can't stay focused long enough to think either thing through. I have tried to hide my memory loss so no one would know how bad it is, but it's gotten to the point where I can't hide it any longer. I become easily confused. Now I am even afraid to drive, because I suddenly get disoriented.[12]

Mood Disorders

As doctors learn more about hypothyroidism, it has become clear to psychiatrists that many of the mental and emotional symptoms of hypothyroidism overlap with the symptoms of depression. It is very common for people with underactive thyroids to become emotionally unstable and depressed. Neurologists are still studying the effects of thyroid hormones on brain chemistry and trying to determine why hypothyroidism and depression so often go hand in hand. Whatever the reason, though, the link is clear. Studies show that more than half of women with low-grade hypothyroidism have experienced major depression at least once in their lives. (About 20 percent of women with normal thyroids have experienced major depression.) When researchers test people who have been hospitalized with severe depression, they find that almost 20 percent of those patients had hypothyroidism caused by Hashimoto's thyroiditis, an autoimmune disease. Because the link between depression and hypothyroidism is so strong, many doctors now feel that it is imperative for all depressed patients to have their thyroid function tested.

Because hypothyroidism can make people so moody, it can also wreak havoc with friendships and relationships. Twenty-five-year-old Angel just wanted to be left alone to sleep. "All I wanted to do was sleep. I couldn't seem to get enough rest," she said later. When her boyfriend, Ted, wanted to spend time with her, she would get angry and irritable: "Ted wanted to take me out to eat, and I didn't want to go. He wanted to go to a movie, and I'd say no. If he rented a movie, I'd just fall asleep. . . . I didn't want to cook or clean. Then he would get frustrated, and I'd get really emotional and mad. He didn't understand that I'm more tired than he is."[13]

Women and Hypothyroidism

Women and girls with hypothyroidism may have an additional set of symptoms. They may suffer from premenstrual syndrome (PMS), irregular periods, or unusually heavy, painful periods. PMS is said to be one of the least understood disorders in medicine, but now researchers are finding that nearly 11 percent of women with PMS also have low-grade hypothyroidism. Some doctors are starting to treat PMS by prescribing thyroid hormones.

If women discuss menstrual problems with a doctor, however, it is likely to be a gynecologist, not an endocrinologist—so the possible connection to a thyroid disorder may be missed. "The most common cause of painful, heavy menses," says Michael, "in the absence of structural abnormalities, is low thyroid. Yet, I have lost count long ago of the women who got hysterectomies . . . who I later diagnosed as being low on thyroid."[14] When she was in her fifties, hypothyroid patient Fran looked back on her decades of irregular periods in amazement:

> Throughout my adolescence and most of my childbearing years, my periods were very irregular. It was not unusual for my cycle to run anywhere from 35 days to 100 days. Then in 1990, at the age of 36, I had surgery for endometriosis and doctors thought that would help make

The most common cause of menstrual cramping in the absence of structural abnormalities is low thyroid hormone output.

my periods regular. It didn't. My hypothyroidism was diagnosed in 1992, when I was 38 years old. This was after 13 years of doctors trying to figure out why I felt so horrible. . . . Finally, in 2001, I asked my doctor if I could try some T3, which I had read about. . . . It never entered my mind that suddenly, at the age of 47, I would start having regular monthly periods for the first time in my life.[15]

Pregnancy and Hypothyroidism

Since thyroid disorders are connected with hormonal imbalances, it makes sense that they would affect not only premenstrual and menstrual problems, but also pregnancy and fertility. It is also common for hypothyroidism to cause periods to become irregular because, like other body processes, the process of ovulation slows down, too. As a result, women with hypothyroidism may find it difficult to become pregnant, because they ovulate less often and have fewer chances to become pregnant. In one study, about 25 percent of women whose doctors referred them to an infertility clinic turned out to have hypothyroidism. Once the hypothyroidism was treated, many of them were able to become pregnant.

Once women do become pregnant, if they continue to have hypothyroidism they have an increased likelihood of miscarriage. This is because hypothyroidism can slow down the process of prenatal development. Thyroid disorders are thought to cause six out of every hundred miscarriages.

Women who did not have a thyroid disorder before becoming pregnant are at increased risk for developing one while they are pregnant or in the first few months postpartum, when hormone levels are fluctuating dramatically. It is easy for doctors to miss postpartum cases of hypothyroidism, though, because women who have just had a baby are expected to be tired and/or depressed. Knowing that between 10 and 15 percent of new mothers suffer from postpartum depression, doctors screen for that, but they may miss the cause of the depression if it is a newly developed case of hypothyroidism. Endocrinologists believe that about 10 percent of new mothers develop thyroid problems. Freelance writer Kristin O'Meara describes what postpartum hypothyroidism felt like:

> I felt like an old woman, and no one knew why. . . . I felt lethargic and groggy, no matter how many naps I took or how well I slept the night before. I knew babies were a lot of work, but I never expected to be as completely worn out as I was. Every morning seemed like a long, slow race to the end of the day, when my husband would come home from work and I could finally sit down.[16]

Since new mothers expect to feel tired and depressed, women with postpartum hypothyroidism typically do not go to see a doctor for their symptoms at all. Twenty-nine-year-old Lisa, who became hypothyroid after giving birth to her second child, did not go to the doctor until she felt so sick that she wondered if she was dying. "I did what women do and I kept going," she wrote later. "I put the smile on when I needed to and I kept up the juggling act the best I could. I started to worry that maybe I was dying from some terminal illness that was going to be discovered too late." Even then she expected the doctor to dismiss her concerns. "I was worried he might think I was a crazy hypochondriac,"[17] she said.

Feeling Crazy

Lisa is not the only hypothyroid patient to assume that the doctor will probably think that she is crazy. In fact, sometimes doctors are skeptical about the vague, random-sounding checklists of symptoms that hypothyroid patients tend to provide. Hypothyroidism is often misdiagnosed or dismissed by doctors who are not sure that anything is really wrong with their patients. Jane, a twenty-eight-year-old nurse who later found out she had hypothyroidism, remembers how this felt: "Being told that nothing was wrong with me made me think I might be crazy."[18] Robert, a vice president at a health care company, felt the same way. He did not want to ask doctors about all his symptoms. "I thought if I asked they'd think I was losing my mind,"[19] he says.

Twelve-year-old Tracy's doctor thought Tracy's mother, Claire, was crazy. "I know my own daughter and I know when

Autoimmune Disorders

Both hypothyroidism and hyperthyroidism are usually caused by autoimmune disorders. These diseases occur when the body's immune system gets mixed up about which parts of the body are healthy body parts and which parts are foreign invaders such as viruses. It is as if the body has become allergic to itself. Hypothyroidism is commonly caused by an autoimmune disease called Hashimoto's thyroiditis, and hyperthyroidism is usually caused by an autoimmune disease known as Graves' disease.

In autoimmune disorders that affect the thyroid, the body's immune system ends up attacking some cells of the thyroid gland. In Hashimoto's disease, antibodies and white blood cells attack and destroy so many thyroid cells that the thyroid gland does not have enough functioning cells to produce as much thyroid hormone as it should, and the thyroid is unable to be as active as it should be. In Graves' disease, which causes hyperthyroidism, the body produces abnormal antibodies that trick the thyroid cells into producing more thyroid hormones than they should. The thyroid is thereby tricked into being more active than it should be.

A patient with Graves' ophthalmopathy, an autoimmune inflammatory disorder affecting the orbit of the eye.

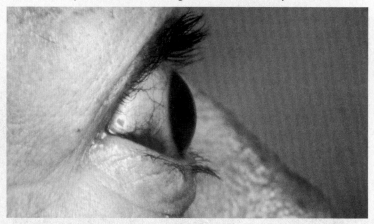

something isn't right," Claire said. Claire, who had hypothyroidism herself, recognized the symptoms when she noticed that not only did Tracy sleep all the time and feel cold, but her hair never grew and her nails never needed to be trimmed. She insisted on a thyroid test. When Tracy's pediatrician received her thyroid test results, he phoned Claire at work. "He said, 'I owe you an apology. Your daughter is very hypothyroid. Her TSH is very high, and she must get to an endocrinologist as soon as possible."[20]

Variations in Severity

Tracy's pediatrician wanted her to see an endocrinologist quickly because her TSH was so high that he feared she would develop severe hypothyroidism. One or 2 percent of the population has hypothyroidism that is so extreme that it threatens their ability to function. People with severe hypothyroidism may develop hypothermia because their body temperatures drop so low. They may become jaundiced or develop swelling of the tissue in their tongues or around their hearts or abdomens. Their speech and movement may slow down. They may become anemic. A few go into a coma. In some cases people with severe hypothyroidism may literally "go crazy" by starting to have hallucinations, paranoid delusions, dementia, or by becoming manic in their behavior.

Most people with hypothyroidism, however, do not develop such severe cases of the disorder. Borderline, or low-grade, hypothyroidism is much more common and affects about 10 percent of the population. Among older people, though, it is even more common. Endocrinologists think that as many as 15 percent of women who are old enough to have gone through menopause have hypothyroidism. About 6 percent of men in the same age range also have underactive thyroids.

Among older people hypothyroidism is often misdiagnosed. When older people develop symptoms like feeling cold and becoming forgetful, people tend to assume that the symptoms are a natural part of getting older. Doctors may assume that elderly hypothyroid patients have dementia or Alzheimer's. Many elderly hypothyroid patients do suffer from dementia,

Starvation and Hypothyroidism

People with hypothyroidism experience many of the same symptoms that affect famine victims, as well as anorexics and bulimics. Anorexia is a disorder in which people, unable to see themselves as they really are, starve themselves in an attempt to become thinner. Bulimia is a similar disorder in which people binge on what they consider to be fattening foods and then throw up to prevent themselves from absorbing the calories from their food. People with anorexia or bulimia often end up literally starving, as if they were famine victims.

When a person begins to starve, the pituitary gland in the brain starts to produce less TSH (thyroid-stimulating hormone). By stimulating the thyroid less, the pituitary can get the thyroid to produce smaller amounts of thyroid hormones. With fewer thyroid hormones to stimulate the body's cells, the cells slow down, and so does the body's entire metabolism. This is the body's way of getting the cells to use less energy, so that the body needs less food. That way the starving person can survive a longer time—hopefully, long enough to have a chance to find food. Like people with hypothyroidism, starving people may feel tired, cold, sleepy, forgetful, and moody and have a hard time concentrating.

but their hypothyroidism may be a contributing factor, which, if treated, could reduce the severity of the dementia symptoms.

Hashimoto's Disease

Patients with hypothyroidism may feel crazy, but in most cases what is really wrong is that they have thyroiditis, an inflammation of the thyroid gland. The thyroid gland can become inflamed as the result of an infection or as a side effect of taking certain drugs. But the most common reason for thyroiditis is

Older people with hypothyroidism are often misdiagnosed with Alzheimer's disease or dementia.

Hashimoto's disease. This is an autoimmune disorder in which the body begins producing antibodies that attack its own thyroid cells. As thyroid cells are damaged and destroyed, it becomes harder for the thyroid to make the needed amount of thyroid hormones. Hashimoto's disease, like hypothyroidism itself, can be diagnosed with a blood test. A lab can test a patient's blood for the antibodies that are produced by Hashimoto's.

Not all patients with hypothyroidism have Hashimoto's disease. Some find that their thyroid function is suppressed after they are exposed to too many goitrogens—foods that suppress the thyroid and stop thyroid cells from producing hormones. Goitrogens include soy products and most cruciferous vegetables such as broccoli, cauliflower, kale, and cabbage.

Getting Treatment

Once hypothyroidism is diagnosed and treated, patients who previously thought they were going crazy may feel a huge sense of relief. Hypothyroidism caused by Hashimoto's disease can usually be treated with thyroid hormones. Many patients must go through a period of adjustment as their doctors tweak the dose and/or the brand of thyroid hormones that are used. In certain cases doctors feel that hypothyroidism can be managed without hormones by making lifestyle changes such as avoiding foods that are goitrogens. Since high levels of stress can affect the body's hormone balance, doctors may also recommend practices that help to reduce stress, such as exercise, meditation, yoga, and massage.

The families of hypothyroid patients may be relieved to hear the diagnosis as well. Peter, the husband of a woman who is recovering from hypothyroidism, wrote that although his wife still needs a lot of sleep, it does not bother him as much now that he understands why. "When I see her slipping away," he says, "I know now what that is about. . . . I think that thyroid patients need a lot of rest, and I encourage her to get it."[21]

Depending on how long hypothyroidism has gone untreated, it can take weeks or months for symptoms to begin to diminish. After about six months, though, most patients feel much better. Lisa, the postpartum mother who expected the doctor to think she was crazy, says that she woke up one day shortly after beginning her treatment and felt "alive." She did not hurt. She made it through lunchtime and still felt fine. "I was going to be living my own life again," she said. "I no longer count how many hours I get to sleep before time to wake up, I just look forward to waking up!"[22]

CHAPTER THREE

Hyperthyroidism: An Overactive Thyroid

Sixteen-year-old James was feeling tired all the time and having trouble concentrating in school. He could not sleep at night and felt like his mind was going in a million directions at once. He felt hot all the time. His family doctor diagnosed him with hyperthyroidism, an overactive thyroid, and prescribed a drug that calmed his thyroid down. Eventually, thinking that he was cured, he stopped taking the drug. His doctor agreed. James later said: "At that point in my life, I had recently finished high school, and all the problems from high school seemed to fall away. I felt like I'd outgrown all that stuff, including my thyroid condition."[23]

But he had not. Four years later James's hyperthyroidism made a comeback. He found himself sweating all the time, even in an air-conditioned room. He felt anxious. His mind kept darting in different directions and he could not focus in his college classes. He was too tired to exercise. "I used to run and lift weights every day," he remembered. "I love exercising. Now I'm too wiped out to do it."[24] Without exercise, James began to gain weight.

Diagnosing Hyperthyroidism

Most people with hyperthyroidism start to show symptoms of it when they are teenagers. But they may not react to those symptoms. Young people like James often tolerate more severe symptoms than older people do, living with their feelings rather than seeking medical treatment. By the time they go to a doctor, the symptoms of hyperthyroidism may have become severe. When James went back to his doctor, his hyperthyroidism was almost missed because he had begun to gain weight; hyperthyroid patients more commonly lose weight. Or more frequently, they lose weight at first, and then start to gain

This cross-sectional CT image view of the neck shows a thyroid nodule, a large round red spot on the right lobe of the thyroid gland (purple).

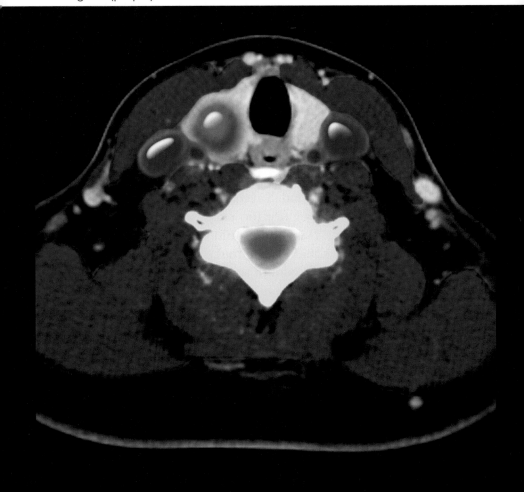

weight later. James may have lost weight in the beginning, but he did not see a doctor then. As a result, it took longer for his doctor to realize that his hyperthyroidism might have returned. When James's TSH levels were finally tested, they had dropped below 0.005 units per milliliter of blood. In 2009 normal TSH levels were believed to be in a range between 0.3 and 3.0 units per milliliter of blood.

Just as high TSH levels make doctors think that the pituitary gland may be trying to stimulate an underactive thyroid, low TSH levels make them think the opposite. The pituitary gland may have drastically reduced the amount of TSH that it secretes, trying not to stimulate further an already overstimulated, overactive thyroid. If this were true in James's case, his doctor expected that further blood testing would show that the levels of the thyroid hormones T_3 and T_4, the hormones made and secreted by the thyroid itself, had risen to very high levels. As it turned out, further testing revealed exactly that. James's symptoms were probably caused by a return of his hyperthyroidism.

James's doctor considered several possible causes for his hyperthyroid condition. One was that he might have nodules growing on his thyroid gland. Thyroid nodules are extremely common, but usually they are too small to be felt. No one knows why they form, but endocrinologists think that about half the population has "hidden" thyroid nodules—nodules too tiny to detect. About 7 percent of the population has nodules that can be felt with the fingers. Thyroid nodules can act as mini-thyroid glands, pumping out excess amounts of thyroid hormones. Nodules can also be a symptom of thyroid cancer. But James's thyroid was smooth and soft. The doctor also considered the possibility that James's thyroid had become inflamed by being infected with a virus (this condition is called thyroiditis). But an infection would probably have made James's thyroid gland tender and swollen, and James did not remember having been sick with a cold or flu. Since he had stopped taking his hyperthyroid medication years earlier, he could not have induced hypothyroidism by taking too high a dose. Ingesting excessive amounts of iodine can also cause the disorder, because thyroid hormones are made of iodine, but James was not ingesting any more iodine than normal. So his doctor thought the most likely diagnosis was the only other option—Graves' disease.

Graves' Disease

Endocrinologists think that between 70 and 80 percent of patients with hyperthyroidism have Graves' disease. Most patients with Graves' disease are women between the ages of thirty and fifty. In fact, Graves' affects women ten times more often than men. But, like James, people can develop Graves' at any age, regardless of gender. Graves' disease is most common in people who have family members with thyroid disorders or other autoimmune diseases and in people who, like James, have a past history of hyperthyroidism.

Like Hashimoto's thyroiditis, Graves' disease is an autoimmune disorder. It occurs when the immune system starts producing antibodies that attack the thyroid gland. Consequently, like Hashimoto's, Graves' disease can be diagnosed by a blood test. Lab technicians can test a patient's blood for the antibodies that are characteristic of Graves' disease.

In Graves' disease, though, instead of damaging thyroid cells themselves (as happens with Hashimoto's), the antibodies attach themselves to the thyroid cells. They attach to the thyroid cells' receptors where TSH is supposed to connect with the cells. Then they stimulate the receptors in the same way that TSH would have—by triggering the thyroid to produce more and more thyroid hormones. The thyroid ends up releasing much higher levels of T_3 and T_4 thyroid hormones than the body needs.

When the thyroid starts producing high levels of T_3 and T_4, the pituitary gland reacts. It stops releasing TSH into the bloodstream, trying to signal the thyroid to stop releasing thyroid hormones. But the thyroid keeps producing hormones in response to the antibodies that are attached to the receptors on its cells. This is why a blood test will usually show that a patient with Graves' disease has low or undetectable levels of TSH in the blood and extremely high levels of T_3 and T_4.

Speeding Everything Up

Doctors do not rely only on blood tests to diagnose hyperthyroidism. In fact, blood tests may end up serving as confirmation of a diagnosis the doctor has already made based on the patient's medical history and symptoms. (It is still important to do the blood tests, though, because it is easy for doctors and patients to confuse hyperthyroidism with other conditions.)

In hyperthyroidism the thyroid gland is overactive and speeds the metabolism up. As a result, people with hyperthyroidism tend to feel very warm or hot, even when they are outside in the cold or in an air-conditioned room. They often lose weight, because it takes a lot of calories to produce enough energy to generate so much heat. As the metabolism speeds up, all the body's processes speed up, too. The digestion may speed up, causing frequent bowel movements or diarrhea. Women may have their periods more often than usual. Children, who are still growing and developing, grow faster and may grow to an unusual height if they develop hyperthyroidism at a young age.

Like other organs in the body, the heart speeds up when it is exposed to large amounts of thyroid hormones. When the heart beats faster, patients may begin to notice frequent heart palpitations. "I thought I was drinking too much coffee,"[25] commented forty-eight-year-old Robert, remembering how he reacted to his own heart palpitations before his doctor diagnosed his overactive thyroid. Jerry, a fifty-one-year-old spinal surgeon and mountain climber, had the same feeling. "You have this constant feeling of being tense, frantic, and irritable, like you will explode at any given minute," he said later. "You feel as though you've had eight cups of coffee and you're just jazzed up all the time."[26]

High Energy

People with hyperthyroidism tend to be very energetic—so full of energy and self-confidence that they seem slightly manic to other people. "I could literally go around the clock," reported Connie, a thirty-four-year-old housewife, "even while I slept. I

A doctor examines a woman's thyroid gland as part of an exam to diagnose a thyroid disorder. Her blood will also be tested.

Hyperthyroidism and Women's Hearts

Heart disease is the leading cause of death for women in the United States, but many women do not realize that they may be at risk. Women with thyroid conditions must be especially vigilant about their cardiovascular health—the health of the heart and circulatory system. Hypothyroid patients must be careful because the weight gain and higher cholesterol levels of hypothyroidism are often associated with heart disease. Hyperthyroidism, though, can be even more dangerous for the heart. According to cardiologist Stephen Sinatra, it can use up the body's reserves of an important nutrient, Coenzyme Q10 (CoQ10). Even women without thyroid problems tend to be low in CoQ10.

"If a woman is hyperthyroid," says Sinatra, "this can be a disaster, because in hyperthyroidism, a hyperactive thyroid gland can burn up all the CoQ10 in the body. The metabolism is so high that CoQ10 is stolen away from the heart." When too much CoQ10 is

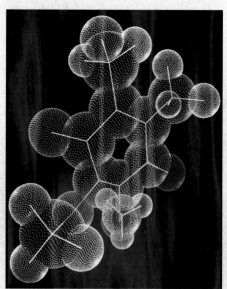

used up, the woman's heart can fail and she could go into a severely hyperthyroid state.

Quoted in Mary Shomon, "Heart Sense for Thyroid Patients: An Interview with Cardiologist Dr. Stephen Sinatra," About.com, December 13, 2003. http://thyroid.about.com /cs/expertinterviews/a/sinatra .htm.

A computer graphic of a molecule of Coenzyme Q 10. Hyperthyroidism can cause a loss of the enzyme from the heart.

could balance my checkbook in my sleep and wake up in the morning and it would be right."[27] People with hyperthyroidism often are happy about this part of the disorder. They feel that they are able to be organized and get things done, and they may feel that they have no need to sleep. Fred, a thirty-one-year-old construction worker with hyperthyroidism, was in awe at his own ability to do several things at once. "The number of things I could keep up with at one time was phenomenal," he says. "I could watch TV, listen to a conversation, eat, and be doing half a dozen other things and keep track of them all like I was intimately involved in every single one of them."[28] Hyperthyroid patients who have this kind of experience may not be diagnosed until they have had the disorder for several years. They feel positive, upbeat, energetic, and see no reason to seek medical help. Fred, for example, had hyperthyroid symptoms for at least four years before he was diagnosed.

Over time, however, hyperthyroid patients begin to see their energy wane, and their optimism breaks apart. Like James, Connie found that her mind was always racing. She was still able to get things done during the day, but increasingly, she could not sleep at night. When she did sleep, her sleep was fragmented—her thoughts kept waking her up. Insomnia is a common symptom of hyperthyroidism.

Anxiety and Stress

The racing thoughts that keep hyperthyroid patients awake at night are part of another symptom of hyperthyroidism: anxiety. Anxiety is almost as typical for hyperthyroid patients as depression is. When thyroid hormone levels are elevated, the rush of adrenaline that might accompany life's normal stresses has a stronger effect on people. As a result, for a hyperthyroid patient, ordinary stress can turn into a panic attack.

Some hyperthyroid patients, rather than becoming anxious, become easily irritated. Mary Lou, a thirty-five-year-old schoolteacher, describes how she began to lose her patience. "Everybody and everything bothered me," she remembers. She stopped teaching Sunday school because she could not keep her temper, and she began to nag her teenage son about everything he did. "He couldn't do anything to satisfy me. If I said, 'take out the trash,' he didn't take it out fast enough. If I said 'put away your clothes,' he didn't fold them fast enough. Everything that happened was surrounded by the word *fast*."[29]

People with hyperthyroidism also will eventually begin to lose their focus and their memory, even if they felt like supermen or superwomen when the disease first began. Connie remembers how her "to do" list started to become less precise. "I felt like a balloon that was about to pop," she says. "My mind was like a computer with no more capacity. It was like there was so much up there, I couldn't decipher one thought."[30]

Psychological Effects of Graves' Disease

Hyperthyroid patients do not always think to tell their doctors about their state of mind. Even if they do share those feelings with a doctor, it may be difficult for doctors who do not specialize in thyroid disorders to distinguish between symptoms that are caused by an overactive thyroid and symptoms that are an ordinary reaction to stress. For example, both stress and an overactive thyroid can cause physical complaints such as heart palpitations, trembling and shaking, and increased frequency of bowel movements. In addition, both conditions can cause mental or emotional symptoms such as anxiety or feelings of panic, which is one of the most common symptoms of hyperthyroidism. Both can also cause restlessness, panic attacks, depression, disorganized thinking, mood swings, aggression, and loss of emotional control.

For Linda, a thirty-six-year-old secretary with Graves' disease, the psychological symptoms began with a series of panic attacks. At random moments in public places, she would become disabled by anxiety, feel unable to breathe, and start having heart palpitations. After four or five months of panic attacks, she began to have other symptoms as well. "It felt like a furnace was burning inside my body," she says. "There were days when I would open the freezer door and put my head in to get relief from the heat intolerance."[31]

During the time period when Linda was having her panic attacks, she ate frequently, had frequent bowel movements, be-

The psychological symptoms of Graves' disease begin with panic attacks.

came nauseated and light headed, lost hair, had night sweats, and began to have bulging eyes. Then her hands began to shake all the time, and she was short of breath. Finally, afraid that she might have muscular dystrophy, she decided to go to a doctor. But the doctor she went to was a neurologist, who told her that all her neurological tests were normal. Linda was not diagnosed with hyperthyroidism until a stranger at a party noticed her glassy eyes and observed that she seemed unusually restless and nervous. The stranger had Graves' disease and asked Linda if she had it as well. Linda decided to find out and went to see an endocrinologist.

Diagnosing Hyperthyroidism

It took Linda an entire year to find out that she had hyperthyroidism. Her experience is typical. It is difficult to make a diagnosis of hyperthyroidism and not all doctors think to check for it with a blood test. Many instead diagnose only the emotional condition, such as depression, that the patient may have developed but do not detect the underlying problem that is causing it. Or doctors react to psychological symptoms by telling patients that they just need to find ways to reduce their stress.

In the late 1990s researchers began to realize that there is a kernel of truth in the advice that doctors have given to so many people with thyroid problems. Stress and thyroid problems are not the same thing, but extreme stress can trigger the development of a thyroid disorder. One study found that stress can increase a woman's likelihood of developing Graves' disease by more than seven times. How can a psychological stress affect the body in a physical way? During extreme stress the hypothalamus gland in the brain releases more of a hormone called corticotrophin-releasing factor, or CRF. This hormone increases the body's alertness and ability to focus and concentrate.

In response to the hypothalamus's release of CRF, the adrenals release the stress hormone cortisol. Cortisol helps the body to respond to temporary stress. But when a person experiences stress all day long for many days at a time, cortisol lev-

The Thyroid Storm

Sometimes undiagnosed, untreated people with hyperthyroidism suddenly go into a medical crisis called a thyroid storm. A thyroid storm occurs when something triggers the thyroid gland to start producing massive amounts of thyroid hormone. The trigger can be an infection, a trauma or accident, surgery (not necessarily to the thyroid gland), a blood clot, or complications from another condition such as diabetes or pregnancy. Going into labor can trigger a thyroid storm in a pregnant woman (but this is rare because pregnant women are screened for thyroid disease).

In a thyroid storm the usual symptoms of hyperthyroidism ramp themselves up to extreme levels. Instead of merely feeling hot, the person in a thyroid storm may spike a 105°F (41°C) fever. Instead of being anxious and moody, the person in a thyroid storm may be psychotic. And instead of operating at faster speeds than usual, the internal organs, including the heart, may simply fail. A thyroid storm is a life-threatening emergency. Fortunately, it is rare, because hyperthyroidism, even though it can be hard to diagnose, is nonetheless usually detected before it reaches such extreme levels.

els remain elevated all the time. One of the things that cortisol does to help the body cope with stress is to provide fuel for whatever needs to be done. Cortisol stimulates the body to release more glucose into the bloodstream and also stimulates the breakdown of fatty acids. During short-term stress, the extra glucose and fatty acids are helpful. They help give a person energy to jump out of the way of a speeding car, for example. After the stress is over, cortisol stimulates the appetite so that the energy that was used up can be replaced.

When cortisol levels are raised permanently or semipermanently, though, glucose levels in the bloodstream also remain permanently high. The body experiences a continually increased appetite, craves carbohydrate foods, and in some

A doctor checks a patient's thyroid gland in her neck as she swallows a mouthful of water. The test will reveal any unusual changes in the size or shape of the thyroid gland.

cases, become resistant to insulin or even diabetic. The immune system becomes weaker, and some doctors hypothesize that this makes the body more likely to develop an autoimmune condition such as Graves' disease. This may be what happened to Ron, who developed hyperthyroidism while living on a military base and working at two jobs while putting his wife through school. He taught classes from six in the morning until three in the afternoon. Then he went to another job, stocking shelves in the commissary, from seven at night until one in the morning. At one of Ron's jobs, his boss was verbally abusive and at home his wife's family was pressuring him to repay some money that he had borrowed from them.

Ron was living in a state of chronic stress and sleep deprivation. He began to lose his temper with the people around him. He became hot and sweaty all the time and developed heart palpitations and insomnia. When he went to a doctor, the doctor told him to see a psychologist to help him deal with his stress. Ron ended up leaving the army when the stress became too much.

Although stress can act as the trigger for the development of Graves' disease, this does not mean that all people who are under chronic stress will develop a thyroid disorder or some other autoimmune disorder. Researchers believe that stress affects a person's brain chemistry in ways that make the development of an autoimmune disorder more likely. But other factors besides stress also play a role. Some people have a genetic predisposition to have a lower tolerance for stress. Others have immune systems that have already been weakened by poor diet, lack of sleep, and/or past illnesses.

Treating Hyperthyroidism

Some cases of hyperthyroidism will improve or resolve themselves on their own. Most cases, though, need some kind of treatment. Leaving hyperthyroidism untreated in the hope that it will clear up on its own is dangerous. It can lead to heart disease or serious psychological disorders such as depression, anxiety disorders, or bipolar disorder. In rare cases a hyperthyroid patient may develop schizophrenia and start having hallucinations or hearing things.

It can be tricky for endocrinologists to decide exactly how to treat an overactive thyroid, however. Overactive thyroid glands are harder to treat than underactive ones. Doctors may prescribe drugs to slow down the release of thyroid hormones. But the choice of drugs and the dose must be customized to the patient. "I did not respond well to the medications," remembers Deborah, a forty-six-year-old hyperthyroid patient. "My symptoms would disappear for a while, then they would return. My doctor kept adjusting my medications, trying to find the right dose."[32]

Another option is radioactive iodine therapy (RAI therapy). Thyroid hormones are made out of molecules of iodine, so people with hyperthyroidism absorb more iodine than the average person. "When you are hyperthyroid from Graves' disease," says Kenneth Ain, director of the University of Kentucky Thyroid Clinic, "your gland is usually quite 'hungry' for iodine."[33] RAI therapy makes use of the thyroid gland's hunger for iodine. The thyroid gland is the only part of the body that uses iodine and therefore is the only part of the body that absorbs iodine. This means that radioactive iodine can be used to target diseased thyroid cells. Unfortunately, radioactive iodine destroys healthy thyroid cells as well as diseased ones. RAI therapy destroys diseased thyroid cells at a much higher rate than healthy ones, though, because diseased cells soak up much more iodine. But it is currently nearly impossible for doctors to determine ahead of time exactly how much radioactive iodine it would take to destroy primarily diseased cells and leave healthy ones mostly intact. RAI therapy tends to turn hyperthyroid patients into permanently hypothyroid ones. But doctors feel that hypothyroidism is safer and easier to treat.

Sometimes doctors will recommend surgery to remove nodules or to remove all or part of the thyroid gland. Removing overactive nodules gives patients some hope that they can recover from thyroid disease and keep the thyroid gland. Like RAI therapy, removing the thyroid gland, or a large part of it, pushes patients into permanent hypothyroidism.

Some hyperthyroid patients have such severe symptoms that doctors prefer to treat the symptoms at the same time as

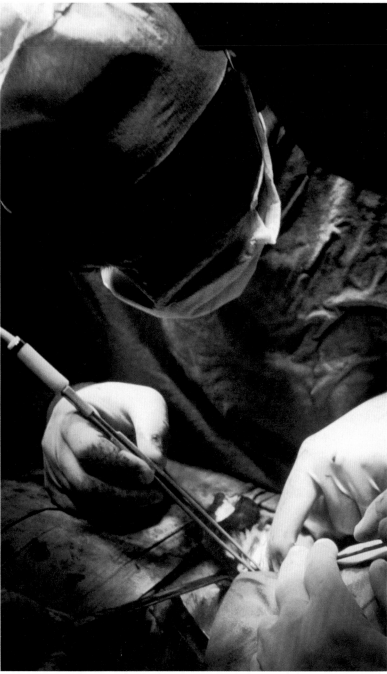

A surgeon performs a thyroidectomy to remove nodules on a thyroid gland.

the disease. For example, patients with a very rapid heart rate may need drugs to lower the heart rate and reduce blood pressure. For reasons that doctors still do not fully understand, some patients develop hyperthyroid eye disease, which causes the tissues behind the eyes to swell, the muscles behind the eyeball to lose some range of motion, and the eyelids to retract. If a patient's eyes are bulging badly, causing double vision or vision loss, doctors may prescribe steroids to reduce the swelling.

Although hyperthyroidism can be tricky to treat, it can almost always be cured, at least temporarily. Even if symptoms return, they can usually be managed so that patients can continue to lead a normal life. Jerry, the spinal surgeon who always felt like he had drunk eight cups of coffee, described how he felt after treatment: "Suddenly, about six to seven weeks after my treatment, I felt better. It happened instantaneously, like someone turned on a switch. Suddenly, I didn't feel as hot. I felt cold. What a good feeling! . . . The best way to describe what I'm feeling now is to say that I had no idea how badly I felt for so long until I was finally able to feel good."[34]

Hyperthyroidism and hypothyroidism are opposites. One is the result of an overactive thyroid, while the other is caused by an underactive one. One speeds up normal body processes, while the other slows them down. Both are typically caused by an autoimmune disease. In hyperthyroidism, though, a substantial minority of cases are not caused by any autoimmune disorder. Instead, they are caused by single or multiple nodules. When this is the case, doctors evaluate the situation with particular care because a small percentage of nodules turns out to be cancerous.

CHAPTER FOUR

Thyroid Nodules and Thyroid Cancer

Nodules are lumps that grow on the thyroid gland. Some nodules are cancerous, but most are completely benign. About half of all people have nodules on their thyroid glands, but usually these nodules are too small to be felt, even by a doctor during a routine checkup. They may not produce any symptoms at all. Sometimes, however, patients with thyroid nodules become hoarse, have difficulty swallowing, or have some pain or discomfort in their necks.

Thyroid cancer is very rare. It represents less than 2 percent of all cancers and 4 percent of pediatric cancers. But because some nodules are malignant, or cancerous, and because some benign nodules later become malignant, doctors evaluate nodules with great care.

Hot and Cold Nodules

Doctors classify thyroid nodules as warm, hot, or cold. About 15 percent of nodules are warm or hot. Hot nodules are not literally hot in terms of temperature. The term "hot nodule" comes from one of the diagnostic tests that doctors do when they are trying to determine whether a nodule is benign or malignant: a radioactive iodine scan (RAI scan). Like RAI therapy, an RAI scan makes use of the fact that diseased thyroid cells absorb io-

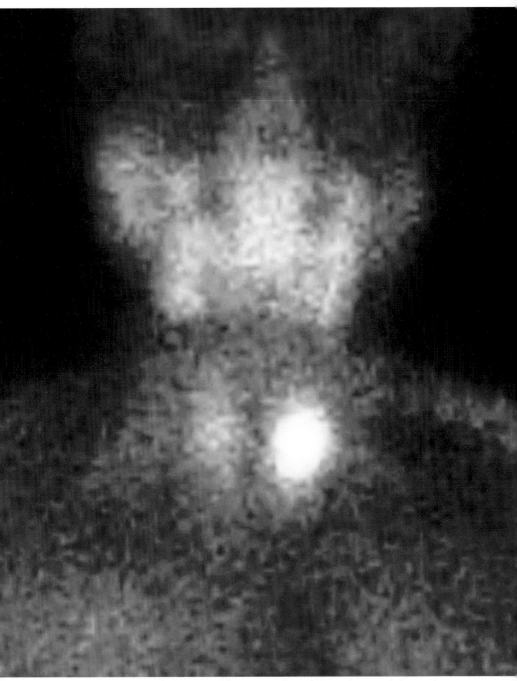

In an RAI scan, a radioactive iodine is used to detect diseased thyroid cells that show up in this X-ray as bright spots in the patient's neck.

dine at a much faster rate than healthy thyroid cells do. The difference between RAI therapy and an RAI scan is the dose—a much smaller dose is used for diagnostic purposes. After the patient takes a dose of radioactive iodine, technicians can take X-ray images of the thyroid. Nodules that absorb unusually high amounts of radioactive iodine will light up when a scan is done. In popular culture, radioactive substances are called "hot," so doctors took to calling these lumps "hot nodules."

Hot nodules are almost never cancerous. They may cause hyperthyroidism, though, because the reason hot nodules absorb so much iodine is that they are using it to produce excessive amounts of thyroid hormones.

Some nodules act like normal thyroid tissue and absorb normal amounts of iodine. These nodules are classified as "warm." Like hot nodules, warm nodules are unlikely to be cancer. Doctors watch them closely, however, and investigate them carefully to make sure that they really are warm and not cold.

When a nodule does not absorb much radioactive iodine, doctors refer to it as a "cold" nodule. About 85 percent of thyroid nodules are cold. Most cold nodules do nothing. They do not produce thyroid hormones and they do not turn into cancer. They just occupy space on the thyroid gland. They are benign.

About 10 to 15 percent of cold nodules, though, are not benign. They are malignant. Almost all thyroid cancer begins as a cold nodule. Patients who have cold nodules should not worry, though, because the vast majority of cold thyroid nodules are benign. But they should follow up with a doctor right away and have more tests done, just in case the cold nodule turns out to be one of the minority that is cancerous.

Checking Nodules for Cancer

When doctors assess a thyroid nodule for the presence of cancer, they must also consider whether the nodule is solid or whether it is a fluid-filled cyst. Thyroid cysts are rarely cancerous, and they rarely get big enough to cause any discomfort or hoarseness. They usually form when a benign solid nodule starts to bleed into itself. If the fluid is drained from a cyst, it will usually go away on its own.

About 70 percent of thyroid nodules are solid. They are made of thyroid tissue and do not contain fluid. Solid nodules are almost never painful. Most are benign, but about 15 percent turn out to be cancer.

To find out if a nodule is cancerous, doctors remove a sample of it in a procedure called a biopsy and send it to a laboratory to be tested. Usually they do a fine needle aspiration biopsy (FNA biopsy). In this procedure, doctors use an ultrasound device to help them guide a long, thin needle into the nodule. Then they withdraw cells through the needle from three to five places in the nodule. About 50 to 75 percent of the time, the FNA biopsy shows that the nodule is benign. Biopsy results can be fairly reliable, but they are not a guarantee. About 3 to 5 percent of nodules that a biopsy shows to be benign are later discovered to be malignant.

Riskier Nodules

Doctors can also predict the likelihood that a nodule is cancerous by looking closely at the size of the nodule and at a patient's medical history and blood test results. A nodule is less likely to be cancer if it is smaller than 0.39 inches (1cm) in diameter or filled with fluid. It is also less likely to be cancer if the patient is pregnant or has hypothyroidism caused by Hashimoto's thyroiditis. A nodule is more likely to be cancer if the patient is male, especially if he is under twenty or over forty. It is also more likely to be cancer if the nodule is bigger than 0.79 inches (2cm) in diameter, rapidly growing, and is hard and solid all the way through, instead of being filled with fluid. A history of radiation exposure to the head, neck, and upper chest or a family history of thyroid cancer, would also make doctors suspect that a nodule might be malignant.

Croatian pro volleyball player Daniel Soric had some of those risk factors when his team doctor found a nodule on his thyroid during a routine pre-signing physical. He was male and the nodule on his thyroid was 2.4 inches (6cm) across and hard. An FNA biopsy showed that the nodule might be malignant. "I felt confident that we would somehow get around this crisis,"[35] Soric remembered later. He was not having any symp-

Terrorism and the Thyroid

On September 11, 2001, terrorists attacked the World Trade Center in New York City, flying planes into the building and causing both towers to collapse. The same day other members of the same group attacked the Pentagon. Another plane was downed by its passengers over a field in Pennsylvania.

In response to the attacks, government officials tried to think of what locations might be attacked by terrorists next and how the nation could prepare for such an attack. Many people were worried that terrorists might attack one of the nation's seventy-four nuclear power plants. Nuclear fallout from an attack on a nuclear power plant, it was thought, could produce a surge of thyroid cancer cases. So in 2002 the Nuclear Regulatory Commission (NRC) began offering potassium iodide pills to anyone who lived near a nuclear power plant. The NRC hoped that if a nuclear disaster occurred, people living near power plants would take a dose of potassium iodide. Their thyroid glands would soak up the potassium iodide, leaving no room to absorb any radioactive iodine that might be released by the power plants in a crisis. People who took a preventive dose of potassium iodide, the NRC hoped, would be able to avoid developing thyroid cancer after being exposed to radiation.

Residents who lived within ten miles of an Illinois nuclear facility received potassium iodide pills in September 2002 in case of a nuclear terrorist attack.

toms, and he felt strong and healthy. Besides, he was about to sign a $1 million, three-year contract with an elite Italian volleyball team, so he needed to be in good health. Soric agreed to have the nodule and half of his thyroid removed. When the lab examined the tissue from the nodule later, it turned out to be benign. But Soric's doctor, Mario Skugor, was still glad that he removed the nodule. "Removing large, hard nodules is standard practice," he said. "They can continue to grow and eventually become malignant."[36]

Thyroid Cancer

Although thyroid cancer is extremely rare, it is also the fastest rising cancer in men and women, faster than lung cancer and breast cancer. The numbers of cancers of all kinds found in the head and neck area have increased by 25 percent over the last thirty years. Thyroid cancer is more common in women than in men. At any given time, about three hundred thousand people in the United States are living with thyroid cancer. Women account for 75 percent of new cases and 58 percent of deaths. Thyroid cancer is the eighth most common cancer in women.

Scientists are not certain why thyroid cancer rates are rising. But they suspect that it is connected with the higher levels of radiation that many people were exposed to during the twentieth century. When people do develop thyroid cancer, it is often a result of exposure to radiation. After the Chernobyl nuclear power plant disaster in 1986, the rate of thyroid cancer, especially in children living near the power plant, rose to one hundred times its normal level. Similarly, thyroid cancer levels rose to one hundred times normal in the Marshall Islands in the Pacific Ocean after atomic bombs were tested there in 1954. The National Cancer Institute has also found that people living in the American Midwest are at higher than average risk (though the risk is still very small) for thyroid cancer, especially if they were children when nuclear weapons were being tested in Nevada from 1951 to 1958, because winds carried fallout toward the east. People are also at higher risk for thyroid cancer if they were exposed to high-dose X-rays to their head and neck as part of a medical proce-

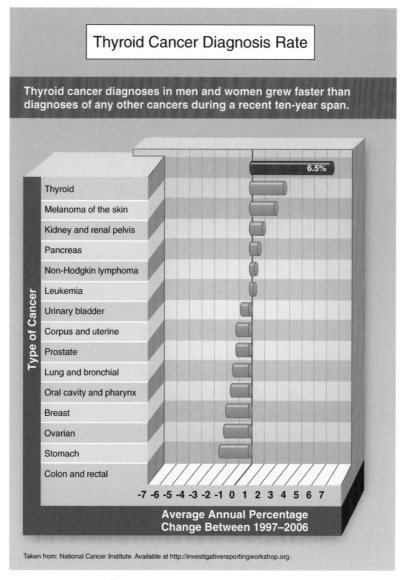

Thyroid Cancer Diagnosis Rate

Thyroid cancer diagnoses in men and women grew faster than diagnoses of any other cancers during a recent ten-year span.

6.5%

Thyroid
Melanoma of the skin
Kidney and renal pelvis
Pancreas
Non-Hodgkin lymphoma
Leukemia
Urinary bladder
Corpus and uterine
Prostate
Lung and bronchial
Oral cavity and pharynx
Breast
Ovarian
Stomach
Colon and rectal

Type of Cancer

-7 -6 -5 -4 -3 -2 -1 0 1 2 3 4 5 6 7

Average Annual Percentage Change Between 1997–2006

Taken from: National Cancer Institute. Available at http://investigativereportingworkshop.org.

dure. Not everyone exposed to high levels of radiation develops cancer, however.

Types of Thyroid Cancer

There are two basic types of thyroid cancer: papillary and follicular. The most common type is papillary cancer, which accounts for about 80 percent of cases. This type of cancer is

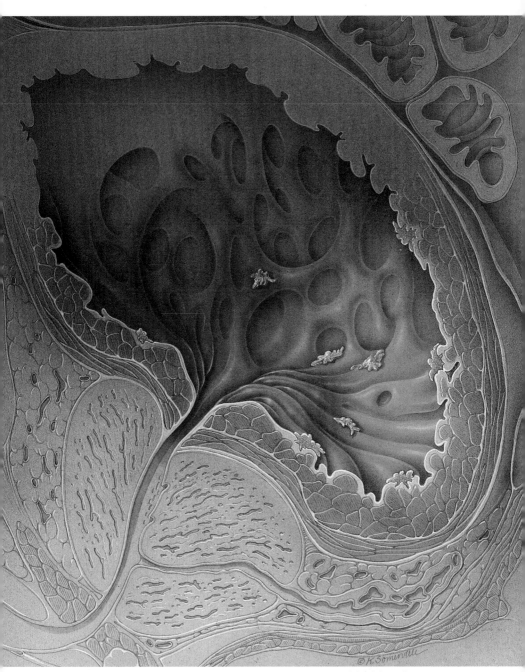

This illustration shows a papillary cancer tumor on a bladder. The most common of thyroid cancers, papillary cancer accounts for 80 percent of cases.

named for its tendency to look like fingers (papillae) under a microscope. Papillary cancer tends to occur in younger people and ordinary papillary cancer is not very aggressive. Two subtypes of papillary cancer—tall cell variant and Hurthle cell variant cancers—are aggressive, however. These cancers can be very invasive and are often harder to detect at early stages.

Another 10 percent of thyroid cancers are follicular, which means that they develop from thyroid follicle cells. This type of cancer tends to occur in older people and is more aggressive and more dangerous than ordinary papillary cancers. Follicular cancers shed cells easily into the bloodstream and migrate from there to distant sites such as the lungs, bones, and liver. Three to 4 percent of thyroid cancers are a special type of follicular cancer called Hurthle cell cancer. (Hurthle cell cancer is different from the variant of papillary cancer that is called Hurthle cell variant.) This type of cancer is much more aggressive. It quickly spreads to the lymph nodes. Another follicular cancer subtype, insular thyroid cancer, is also very aggressive.

Rarer Types of Thyroid Cancer

Three other types of thyroid cancer are even more rare than ordinary thyroid cancer: anaplastic thyroid cancer, thyroid lymphoma, and medullary thyroid cancer. Anaplastic thyroid cancer is the rarest form of thyroid cancer. In the United States fewer than four hundred new cases are diagnosed every year. Anaplastic cancers represent only 1.6 percent of all thyroid cancers. However, unlike most other thyroid cancers, it is very aggressive; in fact, it is one of the most aggressive cancers in existence. Anaplastic cancers grow rapidly, with some doubling in size every two days. They are very difficult to treat. Patients who survive these cancers usually have had a thyroidectomy, very aggressive radiation therapy, and some chemotherapy (using chemicals to kill cancer cells).

Thyroid lymphoma represents less than 3 percent of all thyroid cancers. A thyroid lymphoma is a rapidly enlarging nodule that grows noticeably larger every week or so and takes up half of the thyroid gland or more. Because it grows so fast, thyroid lymphoma is sometimes mistaken for anaplastic thyroid cancer at first. However, unlike anaplastic cancer, thyroid lymphoma can be treated with a combination of chemotherapy and radiation therapy. It usually does not require surgery.

Medullary Thyroid Cancer

Medullary thyroid cancer accounts for about 5 to 10 percent of thyroid cancers. Medullary cancer occurs when cancer develops on the parafollicular cells, which are cells that do not respond to TSH, make thyroid hormones, or absorb iodine. Normal, noncancerous thyroid parafollicular cells make calcitonin, a hormone that stimulates the body to shift calcium and phosphorus out of the blood and use it in the formation of new bone tissue. Medullary cancer cells, though, make carcinoembryonic antigen—a type of protein molecule that is linked to many types of cancer.

Medullary thyroid cancer is incurable. Radioactive iodine therapy (RAI therapy) does not help because the follicular cells of the thyroid do not suck up iodine from the body. Surgery is currently the only option. Fortunately, medullary thyroid cancer develops slowly. People who have this type of cancer have a 90 percent chance of still being alive ten years later if the cancer is still contained in the thyroid gland at the time of the diagnosis. They have a 70 percent chance of surviving another decade if the cancer has spread to the lymph nodes and a 20 percent chance if it has spread to distant parts of the body.

The best way to treat medullary thyroid cancer, endocrinologists say, is to remove the entire thyroid gland before the cancer develops. This is possible in some cases because geneticists have identified the gene that is associated with medullary thyroid cancer. Children with this gene always have at least one parent who developed medullary cancer. Having the gene causes a child to have a 100 percent chance of developing medullary cancer in his or her lifetime. Endocrinologists recommend that children with this gene have thyroidectomies right away, even if they are as young as three years old. Children who have their thyroids removed will have to take hormones for hypothyroidism for the rest of their lives. But

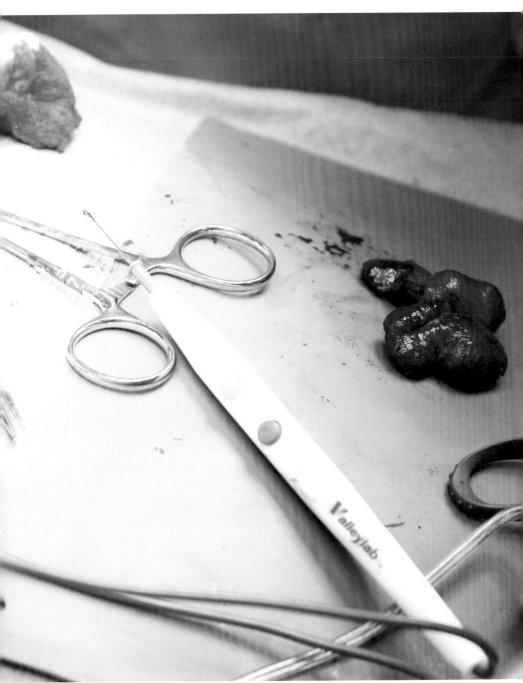

The best way to treat medullary thyroid cancer is to surgically remove the entire thyroid before the cancer develops or spreads.

doctors feel that is a safer choice than waiting and wondering when cancer will develop.

Children with Thyroid Cancer

Children almost never get thyroid cancer. Only about 1.5 percent of children develop thyroid nodules before they reach puberty, and of those, only about one quarter of the nodules turn out to be malignant. It is very important to check thyroid nodules in children when they do appear, however, because on the rare occasions when a child does develop thyroid cancer, the cancer is likely to be very aggressive. Thyroid nodules in children are four times more likely to be malignant than nodules that form in adults. At the same time neither thyroid nodules nor thyroid cancer in children is likely to cause any symptoms, so it is harder for doctors to catch cancerous nodules at an early stage.

Nodules in children are ordinarily only diagnosed if a doctor happens to notice one during a routine checkup. But for thyroid cancer, just as in other kinds of cancer, catching it early is the key to long-term patient survival. When cancer is not caught at an early stage, some cancer cells may break away and enter the blood or lymph fluid. Then these breakaway cells metastasize, or spread, to other parts of the body. Children often do not have their cancers diagnosed until the cancer has already metastasized. About half the time, thyroid cancers in children have already reached the lymph nodes by the time of diagnosis. About 20 percent of the time, children's thyroid cancers spread to distant locations, such as the lungs, before they are discovered. When cancer spreads to the bones or vital organs such as the lungs, the patient's prognosis is not very good.

Treating Thyroid Cancer

Both papillary cancers and follicular cancers are treated the same way, with a thyroidectomy. (Patients with follicular cancer, though, may need to have cancer removed from their lymph nodes as well.) If the cancer is very small and has not spread, a partial thyroidectomy may be enough. It is better to save as much of the thyroid gland as possible, since thyroid hormones play such an important role in regulating the body's

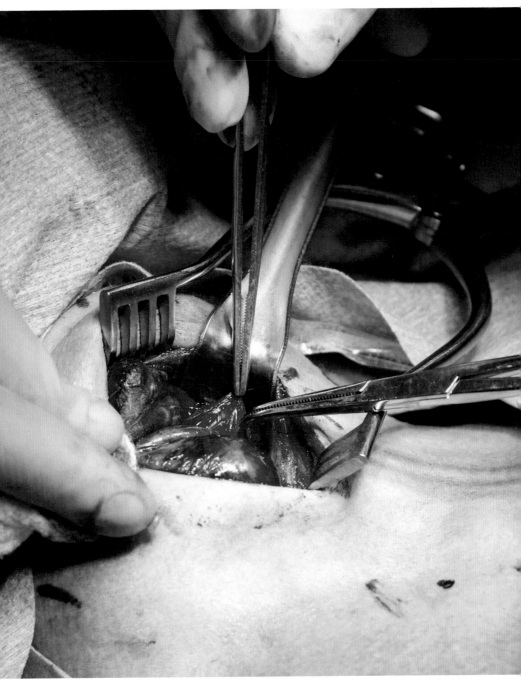

Removal of the thyroid is difficult surgery that may take up to eight hours.

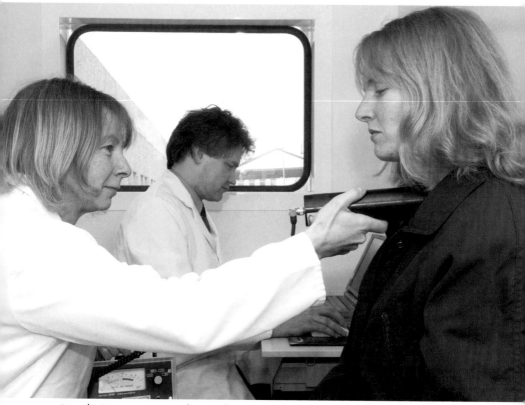

A technician uses an iodine radiation probe to measure the amount of
radiation absorbed by the woman's thyroid gland.

metabolism. If the cancer is larger, though, and/or has spread,
the entire thyroid gland usually must be removed.

Removing the thyroid gland is a very difficult surgery, since
the thyroid is wrapped around the windpipe on three sides.
The surgery usually lasts around four hours, but it can take as
long as eight. Even so, it is nearly impossible to remove 100
percent of thyroid tissue. It is too closely intertwined with
nearby blood vessels and nerves.

To kill any thyroid cancer cells that may remain after a thyroidectomy, patients are treated with radioactive iodine. Doctors
give the patient a liquid containing radioactive iodine and have
the patient drink it. Any remaining thyroid cells, even after a
thyroidectomy, will soak up the iodine. Because the iodine is

radioactive, it will kill the cells that take it in, whether they are healthy or diseased. Most patients have RAI treatment about six to eight weeks after a thyroidectomy. They may repeat it periodically, if follow-up lab work shows that some thyroid cells may still be active in the body.

Removing the thyroid and killing any remaining thyroid cells means that the patient will be hypothyroid for the rest of his or her life. But when the alternative is to let the cancer develop unhindered, most patients feel that removing the thyroid is worth it. However, they must then take thyroid hormones for the resulting hypothyroidism for the rest of their lives.

Outpatient Radiation

Although RAI treatment is extremely effective for treating patients with thyroid cancer, it has become controversial in recent years. Patients undergoing RAI therapy used to stay in the hospital while they received treatment. But now it has become an outpatient procedure. This means that patients, who are slightly radioactive themselves for almost a month after ingesting radioactive iodine, may be exposing other people, including their families, to radiation.

Twenty-nine-year-old Holly Russell-Milstein refused to go home to her children after receiving RAI therapy at Johns Hopkins University Medical Center. Prior to the treatment, her doctor, endocrinologist Paul Ladenson, told her, "It's safe to be around people for a brief period. You don't want to sit on a couch with your daughter for two hours."[37] The National Council for Radiation Protection and Measurement advises patients who have ingested radioactive iodine not to hold children for more than ten minutes a day for the first twenty-one days and to sleep alone for at least a week after treatment. Russell-Milstein, who had four children ranging in age from nine to two, decided it was not worth the risk. "I'd rather live in a box under a bridge than come home to my small children,"[38] she said. She rented a room for twelve days instead.

Ladenson felt Russell-Milstein's precautions were unnecessary. "There are only two things that can go wrong with this treatment," he said. "You can give the wrong dose to the wrong person, or you can drop the container on your foot. It's made of tungsten and extremely heavy."[39] Despite Ladenson's statement, many patients still consider RAI therapy controversial and worry about going home and exposing family members, especially children, to radiation. About 86 percent of patients receiving RAI therapy go home after their treatment. Since thyroid disorders are far more common in women than in men, and the median age of diagnosis is forty-six, many of these patients are, like Russell-Milstein, mothers of young children, who may expect to be held for more than ten minutes per day.

Life After Thyroid Cancer

Most people who develop thyroid cancer are able to go through treatment and therapy, whether they choose surgery, RAI therapy, chemotherapy, or some combination of the three. Most people with thyroid cancer do not die from it. The most common form of thyroid cancer is easily treatable and 95 percent of people who are treated for it survive for at least five years. About 92 percent of people treated for thyroid cancer survive for at least twenty years. Younger patients are more likely to survive, even if the cancer has already spread. So are patients whose cancer is small at the time of diagnosis (less than 1.2 inches, or 3cm, in diameter). Researchers do not know why, but although men get thyroid cancer less often than women, they are more likely than women are to die of it once they do develop it. In 2004, 5,900 U.S. men were diagnosed with thyroid cancer and 620 died. The same year, 17,700 U.S. women were diagnosed with thyroid cancer and 850 died. In other words, 11 percent of the men died, while only 5 percent of the women died.

Despite the high survival rates, though, thyroid cancer patients say that any kind of cancer is scary to have. Emily, a thyroid cancer patient who had RAI treatment, commented, "I always think how it is interesting that, when it is thyroid cancer, everybody thinks, 'It's no big deal because people don't die from it, and if I had to choose cancer, that is what I would choose.' I look at them, and I say, 'Sorry, but I would choose no cancer.' Cancer is cancer."[40]

Thyroid cancer survivors also have to cope with some lifestyle changes. They are likely to have become permanently hypothyroid with the loss of their thyroid glands. As a result, they must take thyroid hormones for the rest of their lives. In addition, thyroid cancer survivors must take suppression drugs to prevent the pituitary gland from secreting TSH. TSH stimulates thyroid cancer cells to grow, and even a thyroidectomy is not likely to have removed all the thyroid cells that could become cancerous.

A few thyroid cancer survivors must also live with complications from their thyroidectomy surgeries. Thyroidectomy is a delicate surgery. One of its risks is damage to the parathyroid glands. These glands sit next to the thyroid gland and secrete hormones that control the calcium levels in the body. If these glands are damaged, calcium levels can fall to dangerously low levels. Some thyroidectomies can also cause nerve damage. Damage to the laryngeal nerves can cause a patient's

Self Check for Thyroid Nodules

People who have a family history of thyroid cancer may want to check their own thyroids occasionally for the growth of nodules. It is relatively easy to examine one's own neck for lumps. All one needs is a handheld mirror and a glass of water. The first step is to find the area of the neck where the thyroid gland is located—the area close to the collarbone. The next step is to take a sip of water, swallow, and watch the neck in the handheld mirror, looking for any bulges. It might be necessary to repeat this step several times. Doing this self check regularly can help people to be familiar with the normal look and feel of their thyroid glands, so that if there is a change, they will recognize it quickly. If anything does seem unusual, it is important to see a doctor and ask to have the thyroid gland evaluated.

voice to be permanently husky. Another possibility is that the vocal cords may be damaged. The vocal cords regulate the flow of air through the esophagus. If both vocal cords are damaged, it will be hard for the patient to breathe. In such cases it is often necessary for the patient to have a tracheotomy, in which a hole is cut in the windpipe just below the Adam's apple, to improve the flow of air through the esophagus.

Fortunately, most nodules on the thyroid gland are not cancerous, and most of those that are can be easily treated. The same is not always true of mood disorders that sometimes accompany thyroid disorders. In the course of brain imaging studies and other research, scientists are learning that thyroid hormones are one of the chemicals that the brain needs in order to function at its best.

CHAPTER FIVE

The Future of Thyroid Research: Brain Chemistry

Fifty-five-year-old Risa had been depressed throughout her childhood and adolescence. When she was a teenager, she says, people never talked about depression. As an adult she saw a psychiatrist who prescribed antidepressant drugs, but Risa had a bad reaction to them. Every month she felt worse.

"I was suicidal," she remembers. "It was awful. I was ready to be committed." Risa finally went to see a doctor who suggested checking her thyroid, and it turned out that she had hypothyroidism. "When I came to Dr. Blanchard and he told me there was something *physically* wrong with me, I cried. It was something legitimately wrong. I was crazy but I wasn't crazy!"[41]

The Gland of the Emotions

Risa's depression was caused by her thyroid imbalance. Like Risa, many thyroid patients experience emotional and psychological symptoms. Some experience these symptoms first, before they begin to notice any changes in their energy levels or body temperature. Doctors are beginning to realize that mental disorders and thyroid imbalances go hand in hand. Some endocrinologists refer to the thyroid as "the gland of the emotions." Thyroid specialist Ridha Arem writes that thyroid imbalance and its resulting depression may be "the common cold of emotional illness."[42]

Approximately 15 percent of people diagnosed with depression have hypothyroidism.

However, patients and doctors alike frequently miss the connection between an underactive or overactive thyroid and a mental condition such as anxiety, depression, or bipolar disorder. Neurologists are just beginning to explore the connection between hormones, such as those released by the thyroid gland, and brain chemistry.

Hormones and Brain Cells

Like other cells all over the body, brain cells rely on the thyroid gland to regulate their metabolism. Cells all over the brain have receptors for thyroid hormones. This means that thyroid hormones can affect the speed at which brain cells operate. They can cause cells in the brain to take in oxygen and glucose more quickly or more slowly. The regions of the brain that have the highest density of thyroid hormone receptors are located in the limbic system—the part of the brain that governs feelings and thoughts. Thyroid hormone receptors are especially concentrated in the hippocampus, the brain's memory center, and the amygdala, the brain's fear center. So thyroid hormones can affect the ability to think, learn, and pay attention and they can be connected with intense feelings in addition to causing physical symptoms. However, doctors still do not fully understand how thyroid hormones affect psychological states.

Researchers have taken several approaches to figuring out exactly how a person's thyroid status affects his or her mental state. One approach is to keep track of the statistics. For example, about 60 percent of people with hyperthyroidism have one or more anxiety disorders, such as generalized anxiety disorder, panic disorder, social anxiety disorder, post-traumatic stress disorder, or phobias. About 15 percent of people diagnosed with depression have hypothyroidism, and it is even more common among depressed patients who do not feel any better when they take antidepressants.

Another approach doctors have used is to try prescribing thyroid hormones to psychiatric patients in cases where nothing else seemed to help. Treatment such as this is experimental. But studies show that thyroid hormones can be very effective in helping people with depression if used in combination with antidepressants. Thyroid hormones seem to make antidepressants more effective for patients whose treatment did not help them when they were taking antidepressants alone. Anxiety patients, however, do not do as well when they are treated with thyroid hormones. In fact, thyroid hormones often cause anxiety symptoms to get worse—just as an overactive thyroid gland does.

Brain Imaging Studies

Once doctors began to see a link between thyroid hormones and mental disorders, they wanted to know more. Neurologists began to do brain imaging studies, in which they took magnetic resonance images (MRIs), functional magnetic resonance images (fMRIs), and positron emission tomography (PET) images of the brains of thyroid patients. MRIs, fMRIs, and PET scans are ways to see parts of the inside of the brain without having to open the brain surgically. Brain imaging technology can show researchers the size and volume of a particular organ in the brain. Images that are taken while a patient is completing a task of some kind can even show researchers what parts of the brain are involved in that task. For example, if a person is using the frontal lobe of the brain to do something, the frontal lobe will light up when an image is taken.

Using PET scans, as well as MRI and fMRI images, researchers confirmed that hypothyroid patients have decreased blood flow and decreased absorption of oxygen and glucose in certain areas of the brain. They found out that a hypothyroid patient is likely to have less activity in his or her amygdala, hippocampus, and several areas of the cortex (the part of the brain that handles complex activities such as social interactions and language use). In the studies that have been done so far, after hypothyroid patients are treated with thyroid hormones, the amygdala, hippocampus, and portions of the cortex light up during the brain imaging scans just as much as they would in a person who does not have a thyroid disorder.

A Shrinking Hippocampus

Neurologists are just beginning to study the interaction of thyroid hormones with brain cells. But they have several theories

Brain Imaging Technology

Neurologists using brain imaging technology to study mental disorders rely on three basic tools: the MRI, the fMRI, and the PET scan. MRI stands for magnetic resonance imaging. MRIs use very strong magnetic fields and pulses of radio-wave energy. The magnetic resonance technology picks up changes in radio signals as they pass through different types of tissue in the brain. An fMRI combines an MRI with activity. Patients do something, such as try to solve a math problem in their heads or watch a sad movie, while the MRI is in progress. Then scientists use computer software to map the changes that occur in the brain as patients experience thoughts and emotions.

PET stands for positron emission tomography. To do a PET scan, doctors inject the patient with a radioactive substance. The radioactive substance can be used to "tag" a particular kind of molecule, such as oxygen or glucose in the blood. Then doctors can use a tool that detects radiation to map those tissues. A PET scan can show which parts of the brain are receiving the most glucose, for example, and at what speed glucose is being metabolized by the brain. It can also show the progress of hormones through the brain.

A patient undergoes a PET scan as a technician monitors the procedure.

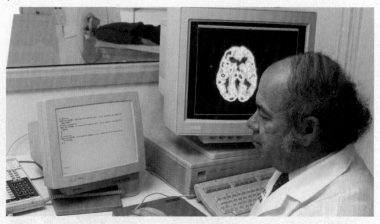

about why thyroid hormones have such a strong effect on the brain. One is that thyroid hormones can affect the size of different parts of the brain. In the brain, cells constantly die and new cells grow to replace them. The process of cell death and cell growth is part of what makes it possible for people to learn new things and adapt to new situations. The brain simply makes new connections.

But cell growth is one of the activities that can speed up or slow down in response to signals from the thyroid. If cell growth slows down in response to the lowered metabolism of hypothyroid patients, it may not be able to keep up with cell death, and when that happens, parts of the brain actually shrink. Lowered metabolism can also lower the amount of oxygen and glucose that brain cells take in, and because cells do not have enough fuel, cell growth slows down even more.

Researchers have measured this shrinkage in brain imaging studies. In depressed patients, the hippocampus, which has the job of making new memories, shrinks—so depressed patients have a harder time learning and remembering new things. So do the frontal lobes of the brain, which are responsible for governing emotions and concentrating attention. Some neuroscientists think that antidepressants may work by increasing the amount of time that thyroid hormones stay in the receptors of certain brain cells, thus encouraging brain cells to grow. When neuroscientists look at the brain images of depressed patients who have been successfully treated, they see that organs in the brain can regain their old size. Many patients completely recover the former size of their hippocampus, for example. Bipolar patients, too, can recover their former brain functions—studies show that after a month of taking medication for bipolar disorder, almost all bipolar patients have an increase in the volume of the gray matter in their brains.

Neurotransmitters

Neurologists have another theory about how thyroid hormones affect the brain as well. Thyroid hormones have been shown to interfere with neurotransmitters. These are chemicals that

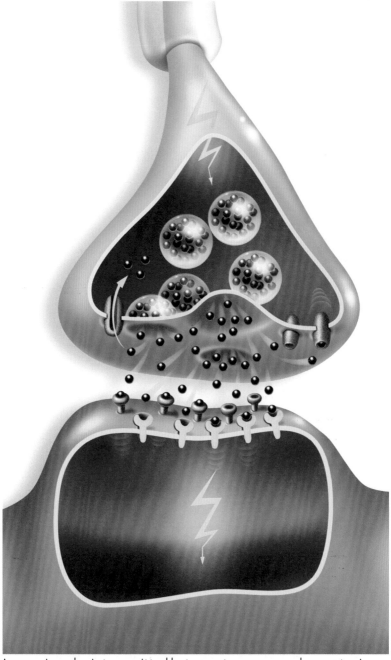

A nerve impulse is transmitted between two synapses by serotonin (maroon balls). The amount of serotonin released is affected by thyroid hormones.

are used throughout the nervous system. They are the signals used by nerve cells to send information across synapses (gaps between nerve cells, so tiny that they can only be seen with a microscope). In the brain, some neurotransmitters can only affect certain kinds of brain cells. Like hormones, neurotransmitters fit into receptors on brain cells. Scientists have identified nearly one hundred neurotransmitters in the brain and suspect that there are many more, each with its own receptors in the brain cells. Each neurotransmitter in the brain has its own functions. For example, one of the most well-known neurotransmitters, serotonin, is found in the hypothalamus and midbrain. It affects mood and hunger as well as some muscle movements. Recent research has shown that when the levels of neurotransmitters in the brain become abnormal, people can become mentally ill. Low levels of serotonin are associated with depression.

Since the late 1990s scientists have conducted hundreds of studies and reviews on the connection between thyroid disorders and depression. Most of this research has centered on effects that thyroid hormones have on serotonin levels in the brain. Researchers have found that serotonin levels are more likely to be normal when thyroid hormone levels are also normal. Neurologists are still not sure why this is so. They know that after serotonin connects with the receptor on a nerve cell, it is reabsorbed by the cells. It may be recycled, or it may be broken down and destroyed. It may be that thyroid hormones slow down the process by which serotonin is reabsorbed, so that it can remain in the synapses a little longer. (That is also how Prozac, an antidepression drug, works.) Or thyroid hormones may act as neurotransmitters in their own right—perhaps serotonin is more effective when it acts in concert with other neurotransmitters. Scientists are not sure, but they hope to find out more in the next few years about how thyroid hormones and serotonin affect each other.

Scientists are also exploring the link between thyroid hormones, neurotransmitters, and degenerative diseases such as dementia, Alzheimer's disease, and Parkinson's disease. Neurologists have known for a long time that patients with severe hypothyroidism develop the same symptoms as elderly patients who have dementia or Alzheimer's disease. Patients who have dementia should always be tested for thyroid disorders, since thyroid disorders are treatable and, if treated early enough, could stop or reverse the progress of the dementia. But scientists are not entirely sure why there is such a strong connection. It could be that other neurotransmitters in addition to serotonin do not function properly unless thyroid hormones are present. Scientists are studying the effects of thyroid hormones on other neurotransmitters such as dopamine, which affects movement and the emotions, and glutamate, which affects memory and learning. Low levels of dopamine are associated with Parkinson's disease, while glutamate irregularities are often associated with dementia and Alzheimer's.

Attention Deficit Hyperactivity Disorder

Many endocrinologists now believe that as a person develops a thyroid disorder, mental and emotional symptoms appear first. But people will live with mental and emotional symptoms for a long time before deciding that they need to tell a doctor. If the person experiencing symptoms is a child or a teenager, parents may assume that he or she is simply acting out or is undisciplined. For example, Cynthia was diagnosed with a rare disorder called thyroid hormone resistance when she was twenty-five years old. She had been having symptoms for a long time, throughout her school years. Cynthia says:

> When I was younger, the teacher would be talking, and I would be off looking at the acoustic ceiling and getting totally lost. Then I would go back, and everybody would be flipping the page, and I would be trying to catch up. . . . Even now, I read two paragraphs and may not even remember what I read because I would be thinking of something else simultaneously. I cannot concentrate on what happens at work or what I'm going to fix for dinner. I'll be driving and not remember having driven to a certain point. . . . At the same time I feel hyper. I can't keep my feet still. I have a lot of energy. All up and about.[43]

Brain Hypothyroidism

In recent years neurologists have begun studying transthyretin, a chemical that can normally be found in the brain and spinal fluid. Transthyretin plays a role in conducting thyroid hormones through the spinal column to the brain. But in depressed patients transthyretin levels are often low. As a result, smaller amounts of thyroid hormones are transmitted to the brain, even if thyroid hormone levels in the blood are normal.

When the transmission of thyroid hormones to the brain is blocked, the result is a condition that some researchers are calling "brain hypothyroidism." In brain hypothyroidism only the brain is low in thyroid hormones. The rest of the body functions relatively normally. Brain hypothyroidism can trigger depression. When it does, the antidepressants that might normally be prescribed often turn out to be ineffective. In cases like this it can be difficult for doctors to diagnose the problem, because blood tests are likely to show that thyroid hormone levels are normal.

As a child, instead of being diagnosed with a thyroid disorder, Cynthia, like many other children and teens, was diagnosed with attention deficit hyperactivity disorder (ADHD). Nobody thought about testing her thyroid function until she became an adult. Today, however, psychiatrists are starting to see the connection. In the late 1990s researchers linked ADHD in children to high levels of thyroid hormones in the blood. One study showed that 70 percent of children with thyroid hormone resistance developed ADHD.

Seasonal Affective Disorder

Thyroid disorders have also been found to play a role in the development of another mental disorder, seasonal affective disorder (SAD). SAD is a disorder that causes people to become depressed and irritable during the winter. People suffering from SAD often have poor concentration and find it harder

Light therapy is effective in relieving the depression that accompanies seasonal affective disorder.

to remember things in the winter than they do in the summer. They may even notice a drop in their physical strength and endurance. Their body temperatures drop and they feel cold all the time. Robert, a vice president at a health care company, had a typical case of SAD. He had been diagnosed with hypothyroidism. His doctor had prescribed thyroid hormones to control his symptoms and he took them faithfully. He was fine until the beginning of winter. Then his symptoms began to come back. Only later did his doctor realize that he had SAD as well as hypothyroidism. "I was falling asleep at the office and praying that no one would walk in when I closed my eyes," Robert says. "One day I even fell asleep on a conference call." He also became extremely depressed. "I'd always been this outgoing energetic funny guy. And I didn't recognize that I became completely antisocial."[44]

New research into the causes of SAD is beginning to explain why so many people, like Robert, have increased hypothyroid symptoms during the winter months. Researchers in Antarctica decided to study SAD, which is thought to be made worse when people are exposed to less light. At the poles, there are times of the year when it is dark all the time. Scientists hypothesized that people living in seasonal darkness would have more extreme symptoms of SAD.

Researchers discovered that many people living at the South Pole develop an extreme form of SAD. They gave this form of SAD the name polar T_3 syndrome, because it comes about when blood levels of the thyroid hormone T_3 drop. The winter darkness of the Antarctic causes thyroid hormone levels of scientists working there to drop significantly.

Depression

If seasonal depression is connected to thyroid disorders, psychiatrists suspected that major depression might be as well. Research showed that they were correct: A strong link exists between hypothyroidism and major depression. Both conditions have similar symptoms: fatigue, mental sluggishness, sleep problems, change in weight, and depressed mood. Both are much more common in women than in men. And treating depressed patients with thyroid hormones often works when nothing else does. In fact, many doctors feel that depression is frequently a misdiagnosis of hypothyroidism. Mike, the husband of a woman with hypothyroidism, writes about how his wife was originally told that what she needed was psychiatric therapy: "They could not find any medical reason for my wife's problems, so they blamed it on pyschosis. The doctor said, 'You need for her to see a psychiatrist.' . . . I know my wife, and I knew that she was not mentally ill . . . she started on the thyroid hormone, and each day I could see improvement in her condition."[45]

According to the Thyroid Society, about 15 percent of depression patients have hypothyroidism. Psychiatrists, though, say that 80 percent of depression patients still suffer unresolved physical symptoms even after their depression has been treated with antidepressants. These patients have symptoms such as weight gain, lethargy, and loss of interest in sex—all of which can also be symptoms of hypothyroidism. Still, treatment with thyroid hormones alone does not usually help these patients—but neither does treatment with antidepressants only. For reasons neurologists are still trying to determine, many of these patients only improve when they take both thyroid hormones and antidepressants. Some psychiatrists think it is likely that in some cases, depression causes the development of hypothyroidism—not the other way around.

Although neurologists are not certain why a connection between depression and hypothyroidism exists, they now think that it may be linked to the effect that thyroid hormones have on the neurotransmitter serotonin. Researchers have recently learned that thyroid hormones regulate the amount of serotonin and several other neurotransmitters in the brain. When thyroid hormones are low, as in hypothyroidism, less serotonin is delivered to brain cells. The same thing is true for several other neurotransmitters. People suffering from depression tend to have low levels of certain neurotransmitters, especially serotonin.

Although treating depressed patients with thyroid hormones produces dramatic improvements for many, doctors caution that this approach does not work for everyone who suffers from depression. "It certainly isn't a magic pill," write Harvard doctors Jeffrey Garber and Sandra White in their book on thyroid disease. "Keep in mind that the symptoms you are experiencing may not be related to the thyroid."[46]

Bipolar Disorder

Just as hypothyroidism is associated with depression, hyperthyroidism is often associated with bipolar disorder. But the connection is not as clear as it is in the case of hypothyroidism and depression. Many bipolar patients with thyroid disorders have

hypothyroidism instead. (Of course, the majority of bipolar patients are not diagnosed with any thyroid disorder at all.) Bipolar disorder is a mental disorder that causes people to cycle between periods when they feel depressed, tired, and lethargic and periods when they are manic, energetic, and impulsive. Studies show that people with bipolar disorder are at much greater risk for thyroid disorders than the rest of the population.

Bipolar disorder causes people to cycle through periods of depression, fatigue, and lethargy, with periods of mania, energy, and impulsiveness.

Patients with rapid-cycling bipolar disorder, in which mood swings may last only hours or days, are at the greatest risk for a thyroid disorder. Studies show that thyroid hormones are very helpful for people with a rapid-cycling form of bipolar disorder, if they are among the subset of bipolar patients who also are not responding to conventional drug treatment. About half of patients whose rapid-cycling bipolar symptoms fail to respond to medication end up being diagnosed with hypothyroidism.

One thing that bipolar disorder and thyroid disorders have in common is that they both commonly start to affect people during the middle school or teenage years. Teenagers who are moody are especially likely to be misdiagnosed. In some cases both bipolar and thyroid disorders may be missed or dismissed as ordinary teenage attitude problems. Sometimes adults suspect teens of taking drugs when they start to see their behavior skyrocket out of control. For example, when twelve-year-old Leslie began having emotional outbursts and sleeping a lot, her parents thought at first that her behavior was just a normal part of growing up and going through puberty. "When everything started showing up," her mother explained later, "it showed up as attitude problems. Until it got severe, being twelve, starting her periods, and going into the teenage years were the ways it was explained." But as Leslie got older, she became even more moody. Her mother described her behavior: "It was like an alien had entered her body. She cried every day. She started doing irrational things that she would never have done in the past. She took acid. I could see her—if it continued—reaching suicide before she reached health."[47]

It took some time for doctors to figure out what was wrong with Leslie. They thought her behavior might be caused by her drug problem. But it turned out that both her behavior and the drug problem were being caused by her medical condition. Eventually Leslie and her family discovered that Leslie had hypothyroidism and rapid-cycling bipolar disorder, which caused her to fluctuate between periods of being up and energetic and periods of being very down and depressed. Her doctors are not certain whether the hypothyroidism led to the bipolar disorder or vice versa. But they do know that when Leslie stops taking her thyroid hormones, her bipolar symptoms flare up. When she takes her thyroid hormones, her mood remains much more stable.

Neurologists are trying to determine what happens to the brain during bipolar disorder. They know from brain imaging studies that the hippocampus, or memory center, tends to shrink in both bipolar disorder and depression patients. But in bipolar patients, the amygdala, or fear center, is often larger than usual. In bipolar patients who have hyperthyroidism, this makes sense. Hyperthyroidism is associated with high levels of anxiety and fear.

Brain imaging technology has given psychiatrists and neurologists many exciting new insights into the brain-thyroid connection. Much of the data, though, is inconclusive. Unfortunately, brain imaging studies are very expensive. Because of the high cost, most of these studies involve a group of about ten or twelve thyroid patients and about ten members of a control group. For a scientific study, that is a particularly small data set. Progress in this field, therefore, is slow and piecemeal—but exciting nonetheless.

Notes

Introduction: A Hidden Cause of Fatigue

1. Quoted in CBS News, "Oprah Reveals Thyroid Trouble," October 17, 2007. www.cbsnews.com/stories/2007/10/17/earlyshow/health/main3377868.shtml.
2. Quoted in Tara Parker-Pope, "Oprah's Thyroid Club," *New York Times*, October 19, 2007. http://well.blogs.nytimes.com/2007/10/19/oprahs-thyroid-club.
3. Quoted in Barbara Rowlands, "The Hormone That Makes You Fat," *London Daily Mail*, September 12, 2006, p. 36.

Chapter One: The Speed Control for the Body

4. Mario Skugor, *Thyroid Disorders: A Cleveland Clinic Guide*. Cleveland, OH: Cleveland Clinic, 2006, p. 8.
5. Jim Phelps, "Thyroid and Bipolar Disorder," PsychEducation.org, September 2008. www.psycheducation.org/thyroid/introduction.htm.
6. Quoted in Paul Ruggieri and Scott Isaacs, *A Simple Guide to Thyroid Disorders: From Diagnosis to Treatment*. Omaha, NE: Addicus, 2004, pp. 20–21.
7. Kenneth Ain and M. Sara Rosenthal, *The Complete Thyroid Book*. New York: McGraw-Hill, 2005, p. xvi.

Chapter Two: Hypothyroidism: An Underactive Thyroid

8. Quoted in Skugor, *Thyroid Disorders*, p. 1.
9. Ridha Arem, *The Thyroid Solution*. New York: Ballantine, 2007, p. 44.
10. Arem, *The Thyroid Solution*, p. 125.
11. Quoted in Mary Shomon, "Getting What You Need from Your Doctor: Challenges of Thyroid Care," *Sticking Out Our Necks*, 2003. www.thyroid-info.com/articles/docdon.htm.

12. Quoted in Arem, *The Thyroid Solution*, p. 45.
13. Quoted in Arem, *The Thyroid Solution*, p. 161.
14. Quoted in Shomon, "Getting What You Need from Your Doctor."
15. Quoted in Mary Shomon, *The Thyroid Hormone Breakthrough*. New York: HarperCollins, 2006, p. 120.
16. Kristin O'Meara, "Kristin's Story: Part I: Getting a Diagnosis," About.com, September 24, 2008. http://thyroid.about .com/library/kristin/blkristin1.htm?p=1.
17. Lisa, "Lisa's Story," Hotze Health and Wellness Center. www.hotzehwc.com/en/cms/?1300.
18. Quoted in Arem, *The Thyroid Solution*, p. 15.
19. Quoted in Ken Blanchard and Marietta Abrams Brill, *What Your Doctor May Not Tell You About Hypothyroidism*. New York: Warner, 2004. Kindle edition, locations 1112–23.
20. Quoted in Jeffrey Garber and Sandra White, *The Harvard Medical School Guide to Overcoming Thyroid Problems*. New York: McGraw-Hill, 2005. Kindle edition, locations 2083–94.
21. Quoted in Arem, *The Thyroid Solution*, p. 169.
22. Lisa, "Lisa's Story."

Chapter Three: Hyperthyroidism: An Overactive Thyroid

23. Quoted in Skugor, *Thyroid Disorders*, pp. 40–43.
24. Quoted in Skugor, *Thyroid Disorders*, pp. 40–43.
25. Quoted in Ruggieri and Isaacs, *A Simple Guide to Thyroid Disorders*, p. 63.
26. Quoted in Garber and White, *The Harvard Medical School Guide to Overcoming Thyroid Problems*, Kindle edition, locations 580–84.
27. Quoted in Arem, *The Thyroid Solution*, p. 68.
28. Quoted in Arem, *The Thyroid Solution*, p. 63.
29. Quoted in Arem, *The Thyroid Solution*, p. 64.
30. Quoted in Arem, *The Thyroid Solution*, p. 62.
31. Quoted in Arem, *The Thyroid Solution*, p. 67.
32. Quoted in Ruggieri and Isaacs, *A Simple Guide to Thyroid Disorders*, p. 55.

33. Ain and Rosenthal, *The Complete Thyroid Book*, p. 168.
34. Quoted in Garber and White, *The Harvard Medical School Guide to Overcoming Thyroid Problems*, Kindle edition, locations 795–99.

Chapter Four: Thyroid Nodules and Thyroid Cancer

35. Quoted in Skugor, *Thyroid Disorders*, pp. 88–89.
36. Skugor, *Thyroid Disorders*, pp. 88–89.
37. Quoted in Steve Sternberg and Anthony DeBarros, "It Kills Thyroid Cancer, but Is Radiation Safe?" *USA Today*, May 28, 2008. www.usatoday.com/news/health/2007-11-18-thyroid-cover_N.htm.
38. Quoted in Sternberg and DeBarros, "It Kills Thyroid Cancer, but Is Radiation Safe?"
39. Quoted in Sternberg and DeBarros, "It Kills Thyroid Cancer, but Is Radiation Safe?"
40. Quoted in Arem, *The Thyroid Solution*, p. 363.

Chapter Five: The Future of Thyroid Research: Brain Chemistry

41. Quoted in Blanchard and Abrams Brill, *What Your Doctor May Not Tell You About Hypothyroidism*, Kindle edition, locations 1139–49.
42. Arem, *The Thyroid Solution*, p. xvi.
43. Quoted in Arem, *The Thyroid Solution*, p. 108.
44. Blanchard and Abrams Brill, *What Your Doctor May Not Tell You About Hypothyroidism*, Kindle edition, locations 1112–17.
45. Mary J. Shomon, *Living Well with Hypothyroidism*, rev. ed. New York: HarperCollins, 2005. Kindle edition, locations 5028-34.
46. Garber and White, *The Harvard Medical School Guide to Overcoming Thyroid Problems*, Kindle edition, locations 537–42.
47. Quoted in Arem, *The Thyroid Solution*, p. 97.

Glossary

amygdala: The brain's fear center.

cell: The smallest living unit in the body. The body's tissues are made of cells, organs are made of tissues, body systems are made of groups of organs, and the body itself is composed of body systems (such as the endocrine system, the digestive system, the circulatory system, etc.).

chemotherapy: Using chemicals to kill cancer cells.

corticotrophin-releasing factor (CRF): A hormone released by the hypothalamus gland in the brain during extreme stress, in order to increase the body's alertness and ability to focus and communicate.

cortisol: A stress hormone released by the adrenal glands to help the body respond to temporary stress.

gland: An organ that produces and releases chemicals that affect the activities of other cells and tissues.

Hashimoto's thyroiditis: An autoimmune disease that causes hypothyroidism.

hippocampus: The brain's memory center.

hormone: A chemical signal that is produced in one part of the body and affects the activity of cells in other parts of the body or throughout the body.

hyperthyroidism: An overactive thyroid—a condition in which the thyroid gland produces larger amounts of thyroid hormones than it should.

hypothalamus: An organ in the middle of the brain that coordinates the activities of the nervous and endocrine systems.

hypothyroidism: An underactive thyroid—a condition in which the thyroid gland produces smaller amounts of thyroid hormones than it should.

iodine: An element used by the thyroid to produce molecules of thyroid hormones.

limbic system: The part of the brain that governs feelings and thoughts.

metabolism: All the chemical processes involved in the synthesis of oxygen and glucose by cells and in the processing of waste; also refers to the speed at which cells and organs function.

neurotransmitters: Chemicals used by the nervous system as signals to send information from one nerve to another across synapses.

nodule: A lump, such as a lump on the thyroid gland.

pituitary: An organ in the center of the brain that makes and releases hormones, including thyroid-stimulating hormone, an important marker for thyroid disorders.

receptor: Places on the outside of a cell where one, and only one, type of chemical can attach itself to the cell and affect the cell's activities. Cells have receptors for hormones, for neurotransmitters, and for many other types of chemicals.

thyroid: The butterfly-shaped gland in the throat that is responsible for regulating the body's metabolism.

thyroid cancer: Cancer of the thyroid gland or thyroid cells.

thyroidectomy: The partial or complete surgical removal of the thyroid gland from the body.

thyroid-stimulating hormone (TSH): The hormone that the pituitary gland sends to the thyroid.

thyroxine: A thyroid hormone that is made of four iodine molecules, also called T_4.

triiodothyronine: A thyroid hormone that is made of three iodine molecules, also called T_3.

Organizations to Contact

American Thyroid Association (ATA)
6066 Leesburg Pike, Ste. 550
Falls Church, VA 22041
phone: (703) 998-8890
fax: (703) 998-8893
Web site: www.thyroid.org

The ATA Web site has articles on new research related to thyroid disorders, including research on how thyroid disorders affect the brain. The site also has printable patient brochures and a "find a specialist" tool.

Graves' Disease Foundation (GDF)
400 International Dr.
Williamsville, NY 14221
phone: (877) 643-3123 (toll-free)
fax: (716) 631-2822
Web site: www.ngdf.org

The GDF Web site has basic information about Graves' disease and treatment options, the campaign to find a cure, and patient conferences. The site also includes meeting times and locations for patient support groups.

Light of Life Foundation (LLF)
PO Box 163
Manalapan, NJ 07726
phone: (877) 565-6325
Web site: www.checkyourneck.com

LLF is an organization dedicated to thyroid cancer patients and survivors. The Web site includes many survivor stories and offers an interface that survivors can use to post their own stories. The site also includes a low-iodine cookbook, thyroid cancer questions and answers, and videos. LLF also runs a thyroid cancer awareness campaign called the "Check Your Neck" campaign.

ThyCa: Thyroid Cancer Survivors' Association, Inc.
PO Box 1545
New York, NY 10159-1545
phone: (877) 588-7904
fax: (630) 604-6078
Web site: www.thyca.org

ThyCa is an all-volunteer group offering support and information to thyroid cancer survivors, families, and health care providers. The Web site includes information about different types of thyroid cancer, a low-iodine diet and low-iodine cookbook, and clinical trials, and it also offers a page of thyroid-related humor.

For Further Reading

Books

Kenneth Ain and M. Sara Rosenthal, *The Complete Thyroid Book*. New York: McGraw-Hill, 2005. A book on conventional treatment for thyroid disorders with more detail than most books on this subject provide. Includes a comprehensive introduction to how the thyroid gland works, information on the parathyroid glands, and an explanation of the different hormones made by the thyroid.

Ridha Arem, *The Thyroid Solution*. New York: Ballantine, 2007. A guide to thyroid disorders with an emphasis on the mental and emotional effects of thyroid disorders. Includes many anecdotes and patient stories illustrating the range of symptoms that can be caused by thyroid disorders and how those symptoms often affect patients' lives.

Ken Blanchard and Marietta Abrams Brill, *What Your Doctor May Not Tell You About Hypothyroidism*. New York: Warner, 2004. A basic book on thyroid disorders, explaining how the thyroid works, how different thyroid disorders affect the body, and what lifestyle changes patients can make to support healthy thyroid function.

Jeffrey Garber and Sandra White, *Harvard Medical School Guide to Overcoming Thyroid Problems*. New York: McGraw-Hill, 2005. A guide for patients who have been diagnosed with thyroid disorders, including clear explanations of how different disorders work. Includes many helpful diagrams.

Gary Ross, *Depression and Your Thyroid*. Oakland, CA: New Harbinger, 2005. A book focusing on the connection between hypothyroidism and depression, including diagnosis, treatment, and the causes of hypothyroidism.

Mary Shomon, *The Thyroid Hormone Breakthrough*. New York: HarperCollins, 2006. A guide to nutritional and alternative approaches to treating thyroid disorders. Includes an extensive index of both conventional and alternative resources, including organizations and Web sites.

Mario Skugor, *Thyroid Disorders: A Cleveland Clinic Guide.* Cleveland, OH: Cleveland Clinic, 2006. A guide to thyroid disorders that explains how each is diagnosed and treated. Includes detailed explanations of tests for thyroid disorders. Also includes a chapter on controversies related to thyroid disorders and topics about which different endocrinologists disagree, such as the role of nutrition and stress in producing a thyroid disorder.

Web Sites

Clinical Thyroidology for Patients, **American Thyroid Association** (http://thyroid.org/patients/ct/volume2/issue2/toc.html). The Web site of the American Thyroid Association's newsletter for patients. Contains articles on recent research related to thyroid conditions, explained in language that can be understood by laypeople.

Metabolism, Rader's Chem4Kids.com (www.chem4kids .com/files/bio_metabolism.html). A Web site meant for kids. Explains what metabolism is and the biochemical reactions that occur when cells metabolize energy from sugar. Includes links to explanations of related topics such as proteins, enzymes, and cell structure. Also includes links to other Web sites that focus on explaining science topics to kids such as Cosmos4Kids (an astronomy Web site), Biology4Kids, Geography4Kids (which focuses on earth science), Physics4Kids, and NumberNut.com (which focuses on math).

Index

A
Adrenal glands, 15, 17
Adrenaline
  hyperthyroidism and, 53
  production in stress
    reaction, *16*
Age, 11
Ain, Kenneth, 29, 60
Alzheimer's disease, 88–89
Amygdala, 83, 84
  in bipolar disorder, 97
Anaplastic thyroid cancer, 71
Anxiety, 53–54
Arem, Ridha, 81
Attention deficit hyperactivity
  disorder (ADHD), 89–90
Autoimmune disorders, 40, 49

B
Bipolar disorder, 59, 94–97
Blood analysis machine, *27*
Blood sugar, 21
Brain, *21*
  thyroid hormones and, 15,
    17, 20–21, 83–84
Brain hypothyroidism, 90
Brain imaging studies, 84, 85,
  97

C
Cancers, *69*
Children

gene for medullary thyroid
  cancer in, 72
iodine deficiency in, 20
thyroid cancer in, 74
Coenzyme Q10 (CoQ10), 52,
  52
Corticotrophin-releasing
  factor (CRF), 56
Cortisol
  in stress reaction, *16*, 56–57

D
Depression, 25, 59, 81, 83,
  92–94
  hypothyroidism and, 35–36
Diagnosis
  of hyperthyroidism, 46–49,
    56–57, 59
  of hypothyroidism, 30–32
  of thyroid disorders, 12–13

E
Endocrine system, 9, *10*, 11,
  15

F
Fine needle aspiration biopsy
  (FNA biopsy), 66
Follicular cancers, 71

G
Garber, Jeffrey, 94

Glucagon, 22
Goiter, 24, *24*
Graves' disease, 40, *40*, 49, 59
  psychological effects of, 54,
    56
  stress as trigger for, 59

H
Hashimoto's thyroiditis, 35,
  40, 42, 44
  hypothyroidism caused by,
    42–44
Heart
  effects of hyperthyroidism
    on, 50, 62
Heart disease, 52
Hippocampus, 83, 84
  in bipolar disorder, 97
Hormones, 9, 15, 17
Hurthle cell cancer, 71
Hyperthyroid eye disease, *40*
  treatment of, 62
Hyperthyroidism, 40
  diagnosis of, 26, 46–49,
    56–57, 59
  symptoms of, 46, 50, 53–54
  treatment of, 59–60, 62
  untreated, 57
Hypophysis gland, *16*
Hypothalamus, 20, 21
  in stress reaction, *16*, 56
Hypothyroidism, 18
  autoimmune, 40
  of brain, 90
  diagnosis of, 25
  in infant, *18*
  misdiagnosis of, 39
  pregnancy and, 38–39

  starvation and, 42
  symptoms of, 32–33
  variations in severity of,
    41–42
  in women, 36, 38

I
Insulin, 21–22
Iodine, 20
  See also Radioactive iodine
    therapy; Radioactive iodine
    uptake scan
Iodine radiation probe, *76*
Iodized salt, 18

M
Magnetic resonance imaging
  (MRI, fMRI), 84, 85
Medullary thyroid cancer, 72,
  74
Metabolism
  effects of hyperthyroidism
    on, 50
  effects of hypothyroidism
    on, 32
  lowered, 86
Michael, Don, 33, 36
Mood disorders, 25
  connection with thyroid
    disorders, 83
  in hypothyroidism, 35–36
Myxedema (hypothyroid)
  coma, 29

N
Nand, Chessy, 12
Nerve impulse, transmission
  of, *87*

Nervous system
  effects of hypothyroidism
    on, 35
  neurotransmitters and, 86,
    88–89
Neurotransmitters, 86, 88–89
Nuclear Regulatory
  Commission (NRC), 67

O
Organ systems, 14–15

P
Pancreas, 21–22
Papillary cancer(s), 69, 71
  of bladder, *70*
Parkinson's disease, 88–89
Pituitary gland, 20–22, *21*
  in hyperthyroidism, 48, 49
  in hypothyroidism, 30
Positron emission
  tomography (PET), 84, 85,
  85
Postpartum depression, 38
Potassium iodide, 67
Pregnancy, hypothyroidism
  and, 38–39
Premenstrual syndrome
  (PMS), 36
Prozac, 26, 88

R
Radioactive iodine therapy
  (RAI therapy), 60, 76–77, 78
Radioactive iodine uptake
  scan (RAI scan), *28*, 28–29
  in diagnosis of thyroid
    nodules, 63, 65

S
Schizophrenia, 59
Seasonal affective disorder
  (SAD), 90, 92
Serotonin, *87*, 88
  depression and, 93
Skugor, Mario, 19
Soric, Daniel, 66, 68
Starvation, hypothyroidism
  and, 42
Stress
  body's reaction to, *16*
  in hyperthyroidism, 53
  as trigger for Graves'
    disease, 59
Symptoms
  of hyperthyroidism, 46, 50,
    53–54
  of hypothyroidism, 32
  of thyroid disorders, 12–13
Synapses, 88
  serotonin in, *87*

T
Thymus gland, 17
Thyroid cancer
  in children, 74
  cold nodules and, 65
  death rates for, 78
  diagnosis of, 66
  diagnosis rate for, *69*
  living with aftereffects of,
    78–80
  prevalence of, 63, 68
  risk factors for, 68–69
  types of, 69, 71–72
Thyroid cysts, 65
Thyroid disorders

prevalence of, 11
screening for, 23, 25
symptoms of, 12–13
See also specific disorders
Thyroid gland, *8*, 8–9
 CT image of, *47*
 growth/development and,
  19–20
 hormones made by, 25
 metabolism and, 17, 19
 radioactive uptake scan of,
  28, 28–29
 RAI image of, 64
Thyroid lymphoma, 71–72
Thyroid nodules, *47*
 biopsy of, 66
 hot *vs.* cold, 63–65
 hyperthyroidism caused by,
  62
 removal of, 60
 self check for, 79
Thyroid Society, 93
Thyroid storm, 57
Thyroidectomy, 60, *61*, 74, *75*,
 76
 complications of, 79–80
 in prevention of medullary

thyroid cancer, 72, 74
Thyroid-stimulating hormone
 (TSH), 22
 blood tests for, 25, 26
 effects on thyroid cancer
  cells, 79
 in hyperthyroidism, 48
 in hypothyroidism, 30
Thyroxine (T_4), 22, 26
 in hyperthyroidism, 49
Transthyretin, 90
Treatment
 of hyperthyroidism, 59–60,
  62
 of hypothyroidism, 44–45
 of thyroid cancer, 74, 76–78
Triiodothyronine (T_3), 22, 26
 in hyperthyroidism, 49
TSH-releasing hormone, 22

W
White, Sandra, 94
Winfrey, Oprah, 8, 9, 11
Women
 prevalence of thyroid
  disorders in, 11
 thyroid cancer in, 68

Picture Credits

Cover: Custom Medical Stock Photo, Inc. Reproduced by permission.
Alfred Pasieka/Photo Researchers, Inc., 52
AP Images, 67
Biophoto Associates/ Photo Researchers, Inc., 18, 40
BSIP/Photo Researchers, Inc., 10, 16, 21, 87
CNRI/Photo Researchers, Inc., 24
Custom Medical Stock Photo, Inc. Reproduced by permission, 13, 51, 64, 70, 73, 75
© Dave Porter/Alamy, 34
© David J. Green–lifestyle themes/Alamy, 31
© Dennis Hallihan/Alamy, 43
Dopamine/Photo Researchers, Inc., 61
Hank Morgan/Photo Researchers, Inc., 85
Ian Hooton/Photo Researchers, Inc., 37
Jim Varney/Photo Researchers, Inc., 27
Lea Paterson/Photo Researchers, Inc., 58
Living Art Enterprises, LLC/Photo Researchers, Inc., 47
Miriam Maslo/Photo Researchers, Inc., 28
Phanie/Photo Researchers, Inc., 55, 94–95
Phillipe Garo/Photo Researchers, Inc., 91
Radiation Protection Division/Health Protection Agency/Photo Researchers, Inc., 76
Richard T. Nowitz/Photo Researchers, Inc., 82
Steve Zmina/Gale, Cengage Learning, 8, 69

About the Author

Bonnie Juettner is a writer and editor with a strong interest in science and health. Her past books for the Diseases & Disorders series include *Skin Cancer* and *Acne*.